Cambridge IELTS 9

*Authentic examination papers
from Cambridge ESOL*

CAMBRIDGE
UNIVERSITY PRESS

CAMBRIDGE
UNIVERSITY PRESS

University Printing House, Cambridge CB2 8BS, United Kingdom

Cambridge University Press is part of the University of Cambridge.

It furthers the University's mission by disseminating knowledge in the pursuit of education, learning and research at the highest international levels of excellence.

www.cambridge.org
Information on this title: www.cambridge.org/9781107615502

First published 2013
3rd printing 2013

Printed in Italy by L.E.G.O. S.p.A.

A catalogue record for this book is available from the British Library

ISBN 978-1-107-61550-2 Student's Book with answers
ISBN 978-1-107-66534-7 Audio CD Set
ISBN 978-1-107-64562-2 Self-study Pack

Contents

Introduction

The International English Language Testing System (IELTS) is widely recognised as a reliable means of assessing the language ability of candidates who need to study or work where English is the language of communication. These Practice Tests are designed to give future IELTS candidates an idea of whether their English is at the required level.

IELTS is owned by three partners, the University of Cambridge ESOL Examinations, the British Council and IDP Education Pty Limited (through its subsidiary company, IELTS Australia Pty Limited). Further information on IELTS can be found on the IELTS website (www.ielts.org).

WHAT IS THE TEST FORMAT?

IELTS consists of four components. All candidates take the same Listening and Speaking tests. There is a choice of Reading and Writing tests according to whether a candidate is taking the Academic or General Training module.

Academic	General Training
For candidates wishing to study at undergraduate or postgraduate levels, and for those seeking professional registration.	For candidates wishing to migrate to an English-speaking country (Australia, Canada, New Zealand, UK), and for those wishing to train or study at below degree level.

The test components are taken in the following order:

Listening 4 sections, 40 items approximately 30 minutes		
Academic Reading 3 sections, 40 items 60 minutes	or	**General Training Reading** 3 sections, 40 items 60 minutes
Academic Writing 2 tasks 60 minutes	or	**General Training Writing** 2 tasks 60 minutes
Speaking 11 to 14 minutes		
Total Test Time 2 hours 44 minutes		

Listening

This test consists of four sections, each with ten questions. The first two sections are concerned with social needs. The first section is a conversation between two speakers and the second section is a monologue. The final two sections are concerned with situations related to educational or training contexts. The third section is a conversation between up to four people and the fourth section is a monologue.

A variety of question types is used, including: multiple choice, matching, plan/map/diagram labelling, form completion, note completion, table completion, flow-chart completion, summary completion, sentence completion, short-answer questions.

Candidates hear the recording once only and answer the questions as they listen. Ten minutes are allowed at the end for candidates to transfer their answers to the answer sheet.

Academic Reading

This test consists of three sections with 40 questions. There are three texts, which are taken from journals, books, magazines and newspapers. The texts are on topics of general interest. At least one text contains detailed logical argument.

A variety of question types is used, including: multiple choice, identifying information (True/False/Not Given), identifying writer's views/claims (Yes/No/Not Given), matching information, matching headings, matching features, matching sentence endings, sentence completion, summary completion, note completion, table completion, flow-chart completion, diagram label completion, short-answer questions.

General Training Reading

This test consists of three sections with 40 questions. The texts are taken from notices, advertisements, leaflets, newspapers, instruction manuals, books and magazines. The first section contains texts relevant to basic linguistic survival in English, with tasks mainly concerned with providing factual information. The second section focuses on the work context and involves texts of more complex language. The third section involves reading an extended text, with a more complex structure, but with the emphasis on descriptive and instructive rather than argumentative texts.

A variety of question types is used, including: multiple choice, identifying information (True/False/Not Given), identifying writer's views/claims (Yes/No/Not Given), matching information, matching headings, matching features, matching sentence endings, sentence completion, summary completion, note completion, table completion, flow-chart completion, diagram label completion, short-answer questions.

Academic Writing

This test consists of two tasks. It is suggested that candidates spend about 20 minutes on Task 1, which requires them to write at least 150 words, and 40 minutes on Task 2, which requires them to write at least 250 words. Task 2 contributes twice as much as Task 1 to the Writing score.

Task 1 requires candidates to look at a diagram or some data (graph, table or chart) and to present the information in their own words. They are assessed on their ability to organise, present and possibly compare data, describe the stages of a process, describe an object or event, or explain how something works.

In Task 2 candidates are presented with a point of view, argument or problem. They are assessed on their ability to present a solution to the problem, present and justify an opinion, compare and contrast evidence and opinions, and evaluate and challenge ideas, evidence or arguments.

Candidates are also assessed on their ability to write in an appropriate style.

General Training Writing

This test consists of two tasks. It is suggested that candidates spend about 20 minutes on Task 1, which requires them to write at least 150 words, and 40 minutes on Task 2, which requires them to write at least 250 words. Task 2 contributes twice as much as Task 1 to the Writing score.

In Task 1 candidates are asked to respond to a given situation with a letter requesting information or explaining the situation. They are assessed on their ability to engage in personal correspondence, elicit and provide general factual information, express needs, wants, likes and dislikes, express opinions, complaints, etc.

In Task 2 candidates are presented with a point of view, argument or problem. They are assessed on their ability to provide general factual information, outline a problem and present a solution, present and justify an opinion, and evaluate and challenge ideas, evidence or arguments.

Candidates are also assessed on their ability to write in an appropriate style.

More information on assessing both the Academic and General Training Writing tests, including the Writing Assessment Criteria (public version), is available on the IELTS website.

Speaking

This test takes between 11 and 14 minutes and is conducted by a trained examiner. There are three parts:

Part 1

The candidate and the examiner introduce themselves. Candidates then answer general questions about themselves, their home/family, their job/studies, their interests and a wide range of similar familiar topic areas. This part lasts between four and five minutes.

Part 2

The candidate is given a task card with prompts and is asked to talk on a particular topic. The candidate has one minute to prepare and they can make some notes if they wish, before speaking for between one and two minutes. The examiner then asks one or two questions on the same topic.

Part 3

The examiner and the candidate engage in a discussion of more abstract issues which are thematically linked to the topic in Part 2. The discussion lasts between four and five minutes.

The Speaking test assesses whether candidates can communicate effectively in English. The assessment takes into account Fluency and Coherence, Lexical Resource, Grammatical Range and Accuracy, and Pronunciation. More information on assessing the Speaking test, including the Speaking Assessment Criteria (public version), is available on the IELTS website.

HOW IS IELTS SCORED?

IELTS results are reported on a nine-band scale. In addition to the score for overall language ability, IELTS provides a score in the form of a profile for each of the four skills (Listening, Reading, Writing and Speaking). These scores are also reported on a nine-band scale. All scores are recorded on the Test Report Form along with details of the candidate's nationality, first language and date of birth. Each Overall Band Score corresponds to a descriptive statement which gives a summary of the English language ability of a candidate classified at that level. The nine bands and their descriptive statements are as follows:

9 Expert User – *Has fully operational command of the language: appropriate, accurate and fluent with complete understanding.*

8 Very Good User – *Has fully operational command of the language with only occasional unsystematic inaccuracies and inappropriacies. Misunderstandings may occur in unfamiliar situations. Handles complex detailed argumentation well.*

7 Good User – *Has operational command of the language, though with occasional inaccuracies, inappropriacies and misunderstandings in some situations. Generally handles complex language well and understands detailed reasoning.*

6 Competent User – *Has generally effective command of the language despite some inaccuracies, inappropriacies and misunderstandings. Can use and understand fairly complex language, particularly in familiar situations.*

5 Modest User – *Has partial command of the language, coping with overall meaning in most situations, though is likely to make many mistakes. Should be able to handle basic communication in own field.*

4 Limited User – *Basic competence is limited to familiar situations. Has frequent problems in understanding and expression. Is not able to use complex language.*

3 Extremely Limited User – *Conveys and understands only general meaning in very familiar situations. Frequent breakdowns in communication occur.*

2 Intermittent User – *No real communication is possible except for the most basic information using isolated words or short formulae in familiar situations and to meet immediate needs. Has great difficulty understanding spoken and written English.*

1 Non User – *Essentially has no ability to use the language beyond possibly a few isolated words.*

0 Did not attempt the test – *No assessable information provided.*

Most universities and colleges in the United Kingdom, Australia, New Zealand, Canada and the USA accept an IELTS Overall Band Score of 6.0 – 7.0 for entry to academic programmes.

MARKING THE PRACTICE TESTS

Listening and Reading

The Answer Keys are on pages 152–161.
Each question in the Listening and Reading tests is worth one mark.

Questions which require letter / Roman numeral answers

- For questions where the answers are letters or Roman numerals, you should write *only* the number of answers required. For example, if the answer is a single letter or numeral you should write only one answer. If you have written more letters or numerals than are required, the answer must be marked wrong.

Questions which require answers in the form of words or numbers

- Answers may be written in upper or lower case.
- Words in brackets are *optional* – they are correct, but not necessary.
- Alternative answers are separated by a slash (/).
- If you are asked to write an answer using a certain number of words and/or (a) number(s), you will be penalised if you exceed this. For example, if a question specifies an answer using NO MORE THAN THREE WORDS and the correct answer is 'black leather coat', the answer 'coat of black leather' is *incorrect*.
- In questions where you are expected to complete a gap, you should transfer only the necessary missing word(s) onto the answer sheet. For example, to complete 'in the ...', and the correct answer is 'morning', the answer 'in the morning' would be *incorrect*.
- All answers require correct spelling (including words in brackets).
- Both US and UK spelling are acceptable and are included in the Answer Key.
- All standard alternatives for numbers, dates and currencies are acceptable.
- All standard abbreviations are acceptable.
- You will find additional notes about individual answers in the Answer Key.

Writing

The model and sample answers are on pages 162–173. It is not possible for you to give yourself a mark for the Writing tasks. For Task 2 in Tests 1 and 3, and Task 1 in Tests 2 and 4, and for Task 1 in General Training Test A and Task 2 in General Training Test B, we have provided model answers (written by an examiner). It is important to note that these show just one way of completing the task, out of many possible approaches. For Task 1 in Tests 1 and 3, and Task 2 in Tests 2 and 4, and for Task 2 in General Training Test A and Task 1 in General Training Test B, we have provided sample answers (written by candidates), showing their score and the examiner's comments. These model answers and sample answers will give you an insight into what is required for the Writing test.

HOW SHOULD YOU INTERPRET YOUR SCORES?

At the end of each Listening and Reading Answer key you will find a chart which will help you assess whether, on the basis of your Practice Test results, you are ready to take the IELTS test.

In interpreting your score, there are a number of points you should bear in mind. Your performance in the real IELTS test will be reported in two ways: there will be a Band Score from 1 to 9 for each of the components and an Overall Band Score from 1 to 9, which is the average of your scores in the four components. However, institutions considering your application are advised to look at both the Overall Band Score and the Bands for each component in order to determine whether you have the language skills needed for a particular course of study. For example, if your course has a lot of reading and writing, but no lectures, listening skills might be less important and a score of 5 in Listening might be acceptable if the Overall Band Score was 7. However, for a course which has lots of lectures and spoken instructions, a score of 5 in Listening might be unacceptable even though the Overall Band Score was 7.

Once you have marked your tests you should have some idea of whether your listening and reading skills are good enough for you to try the IELTS test. If you did well enough in one component but not in others, you will have to decide for yourself whether you are ready to take the test.

The Practice Tests have been checked to ensure that they are of approximately the same level of difficulty as the real IELTS test. However, we cannot guarantee that your score in the Practice Tests will be reflected in the real IELTS test. The Practice Tests can only give you an idea of your possible future performance and it is ultimately up to you to make decisions based on your score.

Different institutions accept different IELTS scores for different types of courses. We have based our recommendations on the average scores which the majority of institutions accept. The institution to which you are applying may, of course, require a higher or lower score than most other institutions.

Further information

For more information about IELTS or any other University of Cambridge ESOL examination, write to:

University of Cambridge ESOL Examinations
1 Hills Road
Cambridge
CB1 2EU
United Kingdom

Telephone: +44 1223 553355
Fax: +44 1223 460278
email: esolhelpdesk@cambridgeesol.org
http://www.cambridgeesol.org
http://www.ielts.org

Test 1

SECTION 1   *Questions 1–10*

Complete the notes below.

Write **NO MORE THAN THREE WORDS AND/OR A NUMBER** *for each answer.*

JOB ENQUIRY

Example
- **Work at:** *a restaurant*

- **Type of work: 1** ....
- **Number of hours per week:** 12 hours
- **Would need work permit**
- **Work in the: 2** .... branch
- **Nearest bus stop: next to 3** ....
- **Pay: 4 £** .... an hour
- **Extra benefits:**
  - a free dinner
  - extra pay when you work on **5** ....
  - transport home when you work **6** ....
- **Qualities required:**
  - **7** ....
  - ability to **8** ....
- **Interview arranged for:** Thursday **9** .... at 6 p.m.
- **Bring the names of two referees**
- **Ask for:** Samira **10** ....

SECTION 2   *Questions 11–20*

Questions 11–16

Complete the notes below.

Write ONE WORD AND/OR A NUMBER for each answer.

SPORTS WORLD

- a new **11** .... of an international sports goods company
- located in the shopping centre to the **12** .... of Bradcaster
- has sports **13** .... and equipment on floors 1 – 3
- can get you any item within **14** .... days
- shop specialises in equipment for **15** ....
- has a special section which just sells **16** ....

Questions 17 and 18

*Choose the correct letter, **A**, **B** or **C**.*

17   A champion athlete will be in the shop

    A   on Saturday morning only.
    B   all day Saturday.
    C   for the whole weekend.

18   The first person to answer 20 quiz questions correctly will win

    A   gym membership.
    B   a video.
    C   a calendar.

Questions 19 and 20

*Choose **TWO** letters, **A–E**.*

Which **TWO** pieces of information does the speaker give about the fitness test?

    A   You need to reserve a place.
    B   It is free to account holders.
    C   You get advice on how to improve your health.
    D   It takes place in a special clinic.
    E   It is cheaper this month.

SECTION 3   *Questions 21–30*

*Choose the correct letter, **A**, **B** or **C**.*

Course Feedback

21 One reason why Spiros felt happy about his marketing presentation was that

    A   he was not nervous.
    B   his style was good.
    C   the presentation was the best in his group.

22 What surprised Hiroko about the other students' presentations?

    A   Their presentations were not interesting.
    B   They found their presentations stressful.
    C   They didn't look at the audience enough.

23 After she gave her presentation, Hiroko felt

    A   delighted.
    B   dissatisfied.
    C   embarrassed.

24 How does Spiros feel about his performance in tutorials?

    A   not very happy
    B   really pleased
    C   fairly confident

25 Why can the other students participate so easily in discussions?

    A   They are polite to each other.
    B   They agree to take turns in speaking.
    C   They know each other well.

26 Why is Hiroko feeling more positive about tutorials now?

    A   She finds the other students' opinions more interesting.
    B   She is making more of a contribution.
    C   The tutor includes her in the discussion.

27 To help her understand lectures, Hiroko

    A   consulted reference materials.
    B   had extra tutorials with her lecturers.
    C   borrowed lecture notes from other students.

28 What does Spiros think of his reading skills?

    A   He reads faster than he used to.
    B   It still takes him a long time to read.
    C   He tends to struggle with new vocabulary.

29 What is Hiroko's subject area?

    A   environmental studies
    B   health education
    C   engineering

30 Hiroko thinks that in the reading classes the students should

    A   learn more vocabulary.
    B   read more in their own subject areas.
    C   develop better reading strategies.

SECTION 4   *Questions 31–40*

Complete the notes below.

Write **NO MORE THAN TWO WORDS** *for each answer.*

Mass Strandings of Whales and Dolphins

Mass strandings: situations where groups of whales, dolphins, etc. swim onto the beach and die

Common in areas where the **31** .... can change quickly

Several other theories:

Parasites

e.g. some parasites can affect marine animals' **32** .... , which they depend on for navigation

Toxins

Poisons from **33** .... or .... are commonly consumed by whales

e.g. Cape Cod (1988) – whales were killed by saxitoxin

Accidental Strandings

Animals may follow prey ashore, e.g. Thurston (1995)

Unlikely because the majority of animals were not **34** .... when they stranded

Human Activity

35 .... from military tests are linked to some recent strandings

The Bahamas (2000) stranding was unusual because the whales

- were all **36** ....
- were not in a **37** ....

Group Behaviour

- More strandings in the most **38** .... species of whales

- 1994 dolphin stranding – only the **39** .... was <u>ill</u>

Further Reading

Marine Mammals Ashore (Connor) – gives information about stranding **40** ....

READING PASSAGE 1

*You should spend about 20 minutes on **Questions 1–13**, which are based on Reading Passage 1 below.*

William Henry Perkin

The man who invented synthetic dyes

William Henry Perkin was born on March 12, 1838, in London, England. As a boy, Perkin's curiosity prompted early interests in the arts, sciences, photography, and engineering. But it was a chance stumbling upon a run-down, yet functional, laboratory in his late grandfather's home that solidified the young man's enthusiasm for chemistry.

As a student at the City of London School, Perkin became immersed in the study of chemistry. His talent and devotion to the subject were perceived by his teacher, Thomas Hall, who encouraged him to attend a series of lectures given by the eminent scientist Michael Faraday at the Royal Institution. Those speeches fired the young chemist's enthusiasm further, and he later went on to attend the Royal College of Chemistry, which he succeeded in entering in 1853, at the age of 15.

At the time of Perkin's enrolment, the Royal College of Chemistry was headed by the noted German chemist August Wilhelm Hofmann. Perkin's scientific gifts soon caught Hofmann's attention and, within two years, he became Hofmann's youngest assistant. Not long after that, Perkin made the scientific breakthrough that would bring him both fame and fortune.

At the time, quinine was the only viable medical treatment for malaria. The drug is derived from the bark of the cinchona tree, native to South America, and by 1856 demand for the drug was surpassing the available supply. Thus, when Hofmann made some passing comments about the desirability of a synthetic substitute for quinine, it was unsurprising that his star pupil was moved to take up the challenge.

During his vacation in 1856, Perkin spent his time in the laboratory on the top floor of his family's house. He was attempting to manufacture quinine from aniline, an inexpensive and readily available coal tar waste product. Despite his best efforts, however, he did not end up with quinine. Instead, he produced a mysterious dark sludge. Luckily, Perkin's scientific training and nature prompted him to investigate the substance further. Incorporating potassium dichromate and alcohol into the aniline at various stages of the experimental process, he finally produced a deep purple solution. And, proving the truth of the famous scientist Louis Pasteur's words 'chance favours only the prepared mind', Perkin saw the potential of his unexpected find.

Historically, textile dyes were made from such natural sources as plants and animal excretions. Some of these, such as the glandular mucus of snails, were difficult to obtain and outrageously expensive. Indeed, the purple colour extracted from a snail was once so costly that in society at the time only the rich could afford it. Further, natural dyes tended to be muddy in hue and fade quickly. It was against this backdrop that Perkin's discovery was made.

Perkin quickly grasped that his purple solution could be used to colour fabric, thus making it the world's first synthetic dye. Realising the importance of this breakthrough, he lost no time in patenting it. But perhaps the most fascinating of all Perkin's reactions to his find was his nearly instant recognition that the new dye had commercial possibilities.

Perkin originally named his dye Tyrian Purple, but it later became commonly known as mauve (from the French for the plant used to make the colour violet). He asked advice of Scottish dye works owner Robert Pullar, who assured him that manufacturing the dye would be well worth it if the colour remained fast (i.e. would not fade) and the cost was relatively low. So, over the fierce objections of his mentor Hofmann, he left college to give birth to the modern chemical industry.

With the help of his father and brother, Perkin set up a factory not far from London. Utilising the cheap and plentiful coal tar that was an almost unlimited byproduct of London's gas street lighting, the dye works began producing the world's first synthetically dyed material in 1857. The company received a commercial boost from the Empress Eugénie of France, when she decided the new colour flattered her. Very soon, mauve was the necessary shade for all the fashionable ladies in that country. Not to be outdone, England's Queen Victoria also appeared in public wearing a mauve gown, thus making it all the rage in England as well. The dye was bold and fast, and the public clamoured for more. Perkin went back to the drawing board.

Although Perkin's fame was achieved and fortune assured by his first discovery, the chemist continued his research. Among other dyes he developed and introduced were aniline red (1859) and aniline black (1863) and, in the late 1860s, Perkin's green. It is important to note that Perkin's synthetic dye discoveries had outcomes far beyond the merely decorative. The dyes also became vital to medical research in many ways. For instance, they were used to stain previously invisible microbes and bacteria, allowing researchers to identify such bacilli as tuberculosis, cholera, and anthrax. Artificial dyes continue to play a crucial role today. And, in what would have been particularly pleasing to Perkin, their current use is in the search for a vaccine against malaria.

Questions 1–7

Do the following statements agree with the information given in Reading Passage 1?

In boxes 1–7 on your answer sheet, write

    TRUE   *if the statement agrees with the information*
    FALSE   *if the statement contradicts the information*
    NOT GIVEN *if there is no information on this*

1 Michael Faraday was the first person to recognise Perkin's ability as a student of chemistry.

2 Michael Faraday suggested Perkin should enrol in the Royal College of Chemistry.

3 Perkin employed August Wilhelm Hofmann as his assistant.

4 Perkin was still young when he made the discovery that made him rich and famous.

5 The trees from which quinine is derived grow only in South America.

6 Perkin hoped to manufacture a drug from a coal tar waste product.

7 Perkin was inspired by the discoveries of the famous scientist Louis Pasteur.

Questions 8–13

Answer the questions below.

*Choose **NO MORE THAN TWO WORDS** from the passage for each answer.*

Write your answers in boxes 8–13 on your answer sheet.

8 Before Perkin's discovery, with what group in society was the colour purple associated?

9 What potential did Perkin immediately understand that his new dye had?

10 What was the name finally used to refer to the first colour Perkin invented?

11 What was the name of the person Perkin consulted before setting up his own dye works?

12 In what country did Perkin's newly invented colour first become fashionable?

13 According to the passage, which disease is now being targeted by researchers using synthetic dyes?

READING PASSAGE 2

*You should spend about 20 minutes on **Questions 14–26**, which are based on Reading Passage 2 on the following pages.*

Questions 14–17

Reading Passage 2 has five paragraphs, **A–E**.

*Choose the correct heading for paragraphs **B–E** from the list of headings below.*

*Write the correct number, **i–vii**, in boxes 14–17 on your answer sheet.*

List of Headings

i   Seeking the transmission of radio signals from planets

ii   Appropriate responses to signals from other civilisations

iii   Vast distances to Earth's closest neighbours

iv   Assumptions underlying the search for extra-terrestrial intelligence

v   Reasons for the search for extra-terrestrial intelligence

vi   Knowledge of extra-terrestrial life forms

vii Likelihood of life on other planets

Example	Answer
Paragraph **A**	**v**

14 Paragraph **B**

15 Paragraph **C**

16 Paragraph **D**

17 Paragraph **E**

IS THERE ANYBODY OUT THERE?
The Search for Extra-terrestrial Intelligence

The question of whether we are alone in the Universe has haunted humanity for centuries, but we may now stand poised on the brink of the answer to that question, as we search for radio signals from other intelligent civilisations. This search, often known by the acronym SETI (search for extra-terrestrial intelligence), is a difficult one. Although groups around the world have been searching intermittently for three decades, it is only now that we have reached the level of technology where we can make a determined attempt to search all nearby stars for any sign of life.

A

The primary reason for the search is basic curiosity – the same curiosity about the natural world that drives all pure science. We want to know whether we are alone in the Universe. We want to know whether life evolves naturally if given the right conditions, or whether there is something very special about the Earth to have fostered the variety of life forms that we see around us on the planet. The simple detection of a radio signal will be sufficient to answer this most basic of all questions. In this sense, SETI is another cog in the machinery of pure science which is continually pushing out the horizon of our knowledge. However, there are other reasons for being interested in whether life exists elsewhere. For example, we have had civilisation on Earth for perhaps only a few thousand years, and the threats of nuclear war and pollution over the last few decades have told us that our survival may be tenuous. Will we last another two thousand years or will we wipe ourselves out? Since the lifetime of a planet like ours is several billion years, we can expect that, if other civilisations do survive in our galaxy, their ages will range from zero to several billion years. Thus any other civilisation that we hear from is likely to be far older, on average, than ourselves. The mere existence of such a civilisation will tell us that long-term survival is possible, and gives us some cause for optimism. It is even possible that the older civilisation may pass on the benefits of their experience in dealing with threats to survival such as nuclear war and global pollution, and other threats that we haven't yet discovered.

B

In discussing whether we are alone, most SETI scientists adopt two ground rules. First, UFOs (Unidentified Flying Objects) are generally ignored since most scientists don't consider the evidence for them to be strong enough to bear serious consideration (although it is also important to keep an open mind in case any really convincing evidence emerges in the future). Second, we make a very conservative assumption that we are looking for a life form that is pretty well like us, since if it differs radically from us we may well not recognise it as a life form, quite apart from whether we are able to communicate with it. In other words, the life form we are looking for may well have two green heads and seven fingers, but it will nevertheless resemble us in that it should communicate with its fellows, be interested in the Universe, live on a planet orbiting a star like our Sun, and perhaps most restrictively, have a chemistry, like us, based on carbon and water.

C

Even when we make these assumptions, our understanding of other life forms is still severely limited. We do not even know, for example, how many stars have planets, and we certainly do not know how likely it is that life will arise naturally, given the right conditions. However, when we look at the 100 billion stars in our galaxy (the Milky Way), and 100 billion galaxies in the observable Universe, it seems inconceivable that at least one of these planets does not have a life form on it; in fact, the best educated guess we can make, using the little that we do know about the conditions for carbon-based life, leads us to estimate that perhaps one in 100,000 stars might have a life-bearing planet orbiting it. That means that our nearest neighbours are perhaps 100 light years away, which is almost next door in astronomical terms.

D

An alien civilisation could choose many different ways of sending information across the galaxy, but many of these either require too much energy, or else are severely attenuated while traversing the vast distances across the galaxy. It turns out that, for a given amount of transmitted power, radio waves in the frequency range 1000 to 3000 MHz travel the greatest distance, and so all searches to date have concentrated on looking for radio waves in this frequency range. So far there have been a number of searches by various groups around the world, including Australian searches using the radio telescope at Parkes, New South Wales. Until now there have not been any detections from the few hundred stars which have been searched. The scale of the searches has been increased dramatically since 1992, when the US Congress voted NASA $10 million per year for ten years to conduct a thorough search for extra-terrestrial life. Much of the money in this project is being spent on developing the special hardware needed to search many frequencies at once. The project has two parts. One part is a targeted search using the world's largest radio telescopes, the American-operated telescope in Arecibo, Puerto Rico and the French telescope in Nancy in France. This part of the project is searching the nearest 1000 likely stars with high sensitivity for signals in the frequency range 1000 to 3000 MHz. The other part of the project is an undirected search which is monitoring all of space with a lower sensitivity, using the smaller antennas of NASA's Deep Space Network.

E

There is considerable debate over how we should react if we detect a signal from an alien civilisation. Everybody agrees that we should not reply immediately. Quite apart from the impracticality of sending a reply over such large distances at short notice, it raises a host of ethical questions that would have to be addressed by the global community before any reply could be sent. Would the human race face the culture shock if faced with a superior and much older civilisation? Luckily, there is no urgency about this. The stars being searched are hundreds of light years away, so it takes hundreds of years for their signal to reach us, and a further few hundred years for our reply to reach them. It's not important, then, if there's a delay of a few years, or decades, while the human race debates the question of whether to reply, and perhaps carefully drafts a reply.

Questions 18–20

Answer the questions below.

Choose **NO MORE THAN THREE WORDS AND/OR A NUMBER** *from the passage for each answer.*

Write your answers in boxes 18–20 on your answer sheet.

18 What is the life expectancy of Earth?

19 What kind of signals from other intelligent civilisations are SETI scientists searching for?

20 How many stars are the world's most powerful radio telescopes searching?

Questions 21–26

Do the following statements agree with the views of the writer in Reading Passage 2?

In boxes 21–26 on your answer sheet, write

> **YES**   *if the statement agrees with the views of the writer*
> **NO**   *if the statement contradicts the views of the writer*
> **NOT GIVEN**   *if it is impossible to say what the writer thinks about this*

21 Alien civilisations may be able to help the human race to overcome serious problems.

22 SETI scientists are trying to find a life form that resembles humans in many ways.

23 The Americans and Australians have co-operated on joint research projects.

24 So far SETI scientists have picked up radio signals from several stars.

25 The NASA project attracted criticism from some members of Congress.

26 If a signal from outer space is received, it will be important to respond promptly.

READING PASSAGE 3

*You should spend about 20 minutes on **Questions 27–40**, which are based on Reading Passage 3 below.*

The history of the tortoise

If you go back far enough, everything lived in the sea. At various points in evolutionary history, enterprising individuals within many different animal groups moved out onto the land, sometimes even to the most parched deserts, taking their own private seawater with them in blood and cellular fluids. In addition to the reptiles, birds, mammals and insects which we see all around us, other groups that have succeeded out of water include scorpions, snails, crustaceans such as woodlice and land crabs, millipedes and centipedes, spiders and various worms. And we mustn't forget the plants, without whose prior invasion of the land none of the other migrations could have happened.

Moving from water to land involved a major redesign of every aspect of life, including breathing and reproduction. Nevertheless, a good number of thoroughgoing land animals later turned around, abandoned their hard-earned terrestrial re-tooling, and returned to the water again. Seals have only gone part way back. They show us what the intermediates might have been like, on the way to extreme cases such as whales and dugongs. Whales (including the small whales we call dolphins) and dugongs, with their close cousins the manatees, ceased to be land creatures altogether and reverted to the full marine habits of their remote ancestors. They don't even come ashore to breed. They do, however, still breathe air, having never developed anything equivalent to the gills of their earlier marine incarnation. Turtles went back to the sea a very long time ago and, like all vertebrate returnees to the water, they breathe air. However, they are, in one respect, less fully given back to the water than whales or dugongs, for turtles still lay their eggs on beaches.

There is evidence that all modern turtles are descended from a terrestrial ancestor which lived before most of the dinosaurs. There are two key fossils called *Proganochelys quenstedti* and *Palaeochersis talampayensis* dating from early dinosaur times, which appear to be close to the ancestry of all modern turtles and tortoises. You might wonder how we can tell whether fossil animals lived on land or in water, especially if only fragments are found. Sometimes it's obvious. Ichthyosaurs were reptilian contemporaries of the dinosaurs, with fins and streamlined bodies. The fossils look like dolphins and they surely lived like dolphins, in the water. With turtles it is a little less obvious. One way to tell is by measuring the bones of their forelimbs.

Walter Joyce and Jacques Gauthier, at Yale University, obtained three measurements in these particular bones of 71 species of living turtles and tortoises. They used a kind of triangular graph paper to plot the three measurements against one another. All the land tortoise species formed a tight cluster of points in the upper part of the triangle; all the water turtles cluster in the lower part of the triangular graph. There was no overlap, except when they added some species that spend time both in water and on land. Sure enough, these amphibious species show up on the triangular graph approximately half way between the 'wet cluster' of sea turtles and the 'dry cluster' of land tortoises. The next step was to determine where the fossils fell. The bones of *P. quenstedti* and *P. talampayensis* leave us in no doubt. Their points on the graph are right in the thick of the dry cluster. Both these fossils were dry-land tortoises. They come from the era before our turtles returned to the water.

You might think, therefore, that modern land tortoises have probably stayed on land ever since those early terrestrial times, as most mammals did after a few of them went back to the sea. But apparently not. If you draw out the family tree of all modern turtles and tortoises, nearly all the branches are aquatic. Today's land tortoises constitute a single branch, deeply nested among branches consisting of aquatic turtles. This suggests that modern land tortoises have not stayed on land continuously since the time of *P. quenstedti* and *P. talampayensis*. Rather, their ancestors were among those who went back to the water, and they then re-emerged back onto the land in (relatively) more recent times.

Tortoises therefore represent a remarkable double return. In common with all mammals, reptiles and birds, their remote ancestors were marine fish and before that various more or less worm-like creatures stretching back, still in the sea, to the primeval bacteria. Later ancestors lived on land and stayed there for a very large number of generations. Later ancestors still evolved back into the water and became sea turtles. And finally they returned yet again to the land as tortoises, some of which now live in the driest of deserts.

Questions 27–30

Answer the questions below.

*Choose **NO MORE THAN TWO WORDS** from the passage for each answer.*

Write your answers in boxes 27–30 on your answer sheet.

27   What had to transfer from sea to land before any animals could migrate?

28   Which **TWO** processes are mentioned as those in which animals had to make big changes as they moved onto land?

29   Which physical feature, possessed by their ancestors, do whales lack?

30   Which animals might ichthyosaurs have resembled?

Questions 31–33

Do the following statements agree with the information given in Reading Passage 3?

In boxes 31–33 on your answer sheet, write

      TRUE   *if the statement agrees with the information*
      FALSE   *if the statement contradicts the information*
      NOT GIVEN *if there is no information on this*

31   Turtles were among the first group of animals to migrate back to the sea.

32   It is always difficult to determine where an animal lived when its fossilised remains are incomplete.

33   The habitat of ichthyosaurs can be determined by the appearance of their fossilised remains.

Questions 34–39

Complete the flow-chart below.

*Choose **NO MORE THAN TWO WORDS AND/OR A NUMBER** from the passage for each answer.*

Write your answers in boxes 34–39 on your answer sheet.

Method of determining where the ancestors of turtles and tortoises come from

---

Step 1

71 species of living turtles and tortoises were examined and a total of **34** .... were taken from the bones of their forelimbs.

Step 2

The data was recorded on a **35** .... (necessary for comparing the information).

Outcome: Land tortoises were represented by a dense **36** .... of points towards the top.

Sea turtles were grouped together in the bottom part.

Step 3

The same data was collected from some living **37** .... species and added to the other results.

Outcome: The points for these species turned out to be positioned about **38** .... up the triangle between the land tortoises and the sea turtles.

Step 4

Bones of *P. quenstedti* and *P. talampayensis* were examined in a similar way and the results added.

Outcome: The position of the points indicated that both these ancient creatures were **39** ....

Question 40

*Choose the correct letter, **A, B, C** or **D**.*

Write the correct letter in box 40 on your answer sheet.

According to the writer, the most significant thing about tortoises is that

    A   they are able to adapt to life in extremely dry environments.
    B   their original life form was a kind of primeval bacteria.
    C   they have so much in common with sea turtles.
    D   they have made the transition from sea to land more than once.

Test 1

WRITING

WRITING TASK 1

You should spend about 20 minutes on this task.

> **The two maps below show an island, before and after the construction of some tourist facilities.**
>
> **Summarise the information by selecting and reporting the main features, and make comparisons where relevant.**

Write at least 150 words.

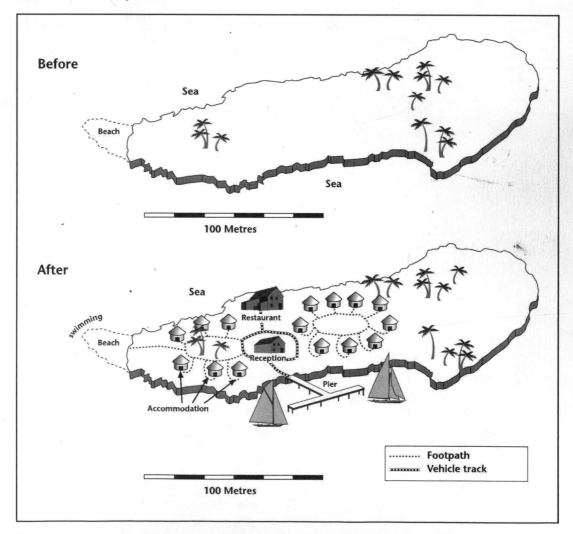

30

WRITING TASK 2

You should spend about 40 minutes on this task.

Write about the following topic:

> *Some experts believe that it is better for children to begin learning a foreign language at primary school rather than secondary school.*
>
> *Do the advantages of this outweigh the disadvantages?*

Give reasons for your answer and include any relevant examples from your own knowledge or experience.

Write at least 250 words.

SPEAKING

PART 1

The examiner asks the candidate about him/herself, his/her home, work or studies and other familiar topics.

EXAMPLE

Games

- What games are popular in your country? [Why?]
- Do you play any games? [Why/Why not?]
- How do people learn to play games in your country?
- Do you think it's important for people to play games? [Why/Why not?]

PART 2

Describe an open-air or street market which you enjoyed visiting.
 	
You should say:
    where the market is
    what the market sells
    how big the market is
and explain why you enjoyed visiting this market.
	You will have to talk about the topic for one to two minutes.
	You have one minute to think about what you are going to say.
	You can make some notes to help you if you wish.

PART 3

Discussion topics:

Shopping at markets

Example questions:
Do people in your country enjoy going to open-air markets that sell things like food or clothes or old objects? Which type of market is more popular? Why?
Do you think markets are more suitable places for selling certain types of things? Which ones? Why do you think this is?
Do you think young people feel the same about shopping at markets as older people? Why is that?

Shopping in general

Example questions:
What do you think are the advantages of buying things from shops rather than markets?
How does advertising influence what people choose to buy? Is this true for everyone?
Do you think that any recent changes in the way people live have affected general shopping habits? Why is this?

Test 2

SECTION 1   Questions 1–10

Complete the form below.

Write **ONE WORD AND/OR A NUMBER** *for each answer.*

Accommodation Form – Student Information	
Example Type of accommodation:	......hall...... of residence
Name:	Anu **1** ....
Date of birth:	**2** ....
Country of origin:	India
Course of study:	**3** ....
Number of years planned in hall:	**4** ....
Preferred catering arrangement:	half board
Special dietary requirements:	no **5** .... (red)
Preferred room type:	a single **6** ....
Interests:	the **7** .... badminton

Priorities in choice of hall:	to be with other students who are **8** ....
	to live outside the **9** ....
	to have a **10** .... area for socialising
Contact phone number:	667549

SECTION 2   *Questions 11–20*

Questions 11–13

Complete the table below.

Write **NO MORE THAN THREE WORDS** *for each answer.*

Parks and open spaces

Name of place	Of particular interest	Open
Halland Common	source of River Ouse	24 hours
Holt Island	many different 11	between **12** .... and ....
Longfield Country Park	reconstruction of a 2,000-year-old 13 ....with activities for children	daylight hours

Questions 14–16

Choose the correct letter, A, B or C.

Longfield Park

14   As part of Monday's activity, visitors will

    A   prepare food with herbs.
    B   meet a well-known herbalist.
    C   dye cloth with herbs.

15   For the activity on Wednesday,

    A   only group bookings are accepted.
    B   visitors should book in advance.
    C   attendance is free.

16   For the activity on Saturday, visitors should

    A   come in suitable clothing.
    B   make sure they are able to stay for the whole day.
    C   tell the rangers before the event what they wish to do.

Questions 17–20

Label the map below.

*Write the correct letter, **A–I**, next to questions 17–20.*

Hinchingbrooke Park

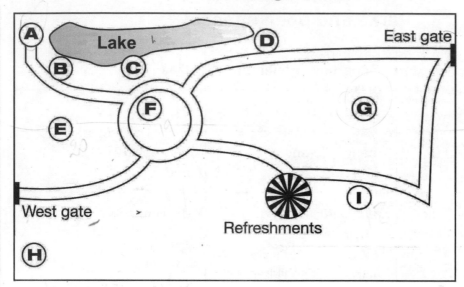

17	bird hide	....
18	dog-walking area	....
19	flower garden	....
20	wooded area	....

SECTION 3   *Questions 21–30*

Questions 21–24

Choose the correct letter, A, B or C.

Self-Access Centre

21 Students want to keep the Self-Access Centre because

    A   they enjoy the variety of equipment.
    B   they like being able to work on their own.
    C   it is an important part of their studies.

22 Some teachers would prefer to

    A   close the Self-Access Centre.
    B   move the Self-Access Centre elsewhere.
    C   restrict access to the Self-Access Centre.

23 The students' main concern about using the library would be

    A   the size of the library.
    B   difficulty in getting help.
    C   the lack of materials.

24 The Director of Studies is concerned about

    A   the cost of upgrading the centre.
    B   the lack of space in the centre.
    C   the difficulty in supervising the centre.

Questions 25–30

Complete the notes below.

Write **NO MORE THAN TWO WORDS** *for each answer.*

Necessary improvements to the existing Self-Access Centre

Equipment

Replace computers to create more space.

Resources

The level of the **25** .... materials, in particular, should be more clearly shown.

Update the **26** .... collection.

Buy some **27** .... and divide them up.

Use of the room

Speak to the teachers and organise a **28** .... for supervising the centre.

Install an **29** ....

Restrict personal use of **30** .... on computers.

SECTION 4   *Questions 31–40*

Complete the notes below.

Write ONE WORD ONLY for each answer.

Business Cultures

Power culture

Characteristics of organisation
- small
- **31** .... power source
- few rules and procedures
- communication by **32** ....

Advantage:
- can act quickly

Disadvantage:
- might not act **33** ....

Suitable employee:
- not afraid of **34** ....
- doesn't need job security

Role culture

Characteristics of organisation:
- large, many **35** ....
- specialised departments
- rules and procedure, e.g. job **36** .... and rules for discipline

---

Advantages:	• economies of scale • successful when **37** .... ability is important
Disadvantages:	• slow to see when **38** .... is needed • slow to react
Suitable employee:	• values security • doesn't want **39** ....

Task culture

Characteristics of organisation:	• project orientated • in competitive market or making product with short life • a lot of delegation
Advantage:	• **40** ....
Disadvantages:	• no economies of scale or special expertise
Suitable employee:	• likes to work in groups

READING

READING PASSAGE 1

*You should spend about 20 minutes on **Questions 1–13**, which are based on Reading Passage 1 below.*

A Hearing impairment or other auditory function deficit in young children can have a major impact on their development of speech and communication, resulting in a detrimental effect on their ability to learn at school. This is likely to have major consequences for the individual and the population as a whole. The New Zealand Ministry of Health has found from research carried out over two decades that 6–10% of children in that country are affected by hearing loss.

B A preliminary study in New Zealand has shown that classroom noise presents a major concern for teachers and pupils. Modern teaching practices, the organisation of desks in the classroom, poor classroom acoustics, and mechanical means of ventilation such as air-conditioning units all contribute to the number of children unable to comprehend the teacher's voice. Education researchers Nelson and Soli have also suggested that recent trends in learning often involve collaborative interaction of multiple minds and tools as much as individual possession of information. This all amounts to heightened activity and noise levels, which have the potential to be particularly serious for children experiencing auditory function deficit. Noise in classrooms can only exacerbate their difficulty in comprehending and processing verbal communication with other children and instructions from the teacher.

C Children with auditory function deficit are potentially failing to learn to their maximum potential because of noise levels generated in classrooms. The effects of noise on the ability of children to learn effectively in typical classroom environments are now the subject of increasing concern. The International Institute of Noise Control Engineering (I–INCE), on the advice of the World Health Organization, has established an international working party, which includes New Zealand, to evaluate noise and reverberation control for school rooms.

D While the detrimental effects of noise in classroom situations are not limited to children experiencing disability, those with a disability that affects their processing of speech and verbal communication could be extremely vulnerable. The auditory function deficits in question include hearing impairment, autistic spectrum disorders (ASD) and attention deficit disorders (ADD/ADHD).

E Autism is considered a neurological and genetic life-long disorder that causes discrepancies in the way information is processed. This disorder is characterised by interlinking problems with social imagination, social communication and social interaction. According to Janzen, this affects the ability to understand and relate in typical ways to people, understand events and objects in the environment, and understand or respond to sensory stimuli. Autism does not allow learning or thinking in the same ways as in children who are developing normally.

Autistic spectrum disorders often result in major difficulties in comprehending verbal information and speech processing. Those experiencing these disorders often find sounds such as crowd noise and the noise generated by machinery painful and distressing. This is difficult to scientifically quantify as such extra-sensory stimuli vary greatly from one autistic individual to another. But a child who finds any type of noise in their classroom or learning space intrusive is likely to be adversely affected in their ability to process information.

F   The attention deficit disorders are indicative of neurological and genetic disorders and are characterised by difficulties with sustaining attention, effort and persistence, organisation skills and disinhibition. Children experiencing these disorders find it difficult to screen out unimportant information, and focus on everything in the environment rather than attending to a single activity. Background noise in the classroom becomes a major distraction, which can affect their ability to concentrate.

G   Children experiencing an auditory function deficit can often find speech and communication very difficult to isolate and process when set against high levels of background noise. These levels come from outside activities that penetrate the classroom structure, from teaching activities, and other noise generated inside, which can be exacerbated by room reverberation. Strategies are needed to obtain the optimum classroom construction and perhaps a change in classroom culture and methods of teaching. In particular, the effects of noisy classrooms and activities on those experiencing disabilities in the form of auditory function deficit need thorough investigation. It is probable that many undiagnosed children exist in the education system with 'invisible' disabilities. Their needs are less likely to be met than those of children with known disabilities.

H   The New Zealand Government has developed a New Zealand Disability Strategy and has embarked on a wide-ranging consultation process. The strategy recognises that people experiencing disability face significant barriers in achieving a full quality of life in areas such as attitude, education, employment and access to services. Objective 3 of the New Zealand Disability Strategy is to 'Provide the Best Education for Disabled People' by improving education so that all children, youth learners and adult learners will have equal opportunities to learn and develop within their already existing local school. For a successful education, the learning environment is vitally significant, so any effort to improve this is likely to be of great benefit to all children, but especially to those with auditory function disabilities.

I   A number of countries are already in the process of formulating their own standards for the control and reduction of classroom noise. New Zealand will probably follow their example. The literature to date on noise in school rooms appears to focus on the effects on schoolchildren in general, their teachers and the hearing impaired. Only limited attention appears to have been given to those students experiencing the other disabilities involving auditory function deficit. It is imperative that the needs of these children are taken into account in the setting of appropriate international standards to be promulgated in future.

Questions 1–6

Reading Passage 1 has nine sections, **A–I**.

Which section contains the following information?

*Write the correct letter, **A–I**, in boxes 1–6 on your answer sheet.*

1   an account of a national policy initiative

2   a description of a global team effort

3   a hypothesis as to one reason behind the growth in classroom noise

4   a demand for suitable worldwide regulations

5   a list of medical conditions which place some children more at risk from noise than others

6   the estimated proportion of children in New Zealand with auditory problems

Questions 7–10

Answer the questions below.

Choose **NO MORE THAN TWO WORDS AND/OR A NUMBER** from the passage for each answer.

Write your answers in boxes 7–10 on your answer sheet.

7   For what period of time has hearing loss in schoolchildren been studied in New Zealand?

8   In addition to machinery noise, what other type of noise can upset children with autism?

9   What term is used to describe the hearing problems of schoolchildren which have not been diagnosed?

10   What part of the New Zealand Disability Strategy aims to give schoolchildren equal opportunity?

Questions 11 and 12

Choose **TWO** letters, **A–F**.

Write the correct letters in boxes 11 and 12 on your answer sheet.

The list below includes factors contributing to classroom noise.

Which **TWO** are mentioned by the writer of the passage?

   A   current teaching methods
   B   echoing corridors
   C   cooling systems
   D   large class sizes
   E   loud-voiced teachers
   F   playground games

Question 13

Choose the correct letter, **A**, **B**, **C** or **D**.

Write the correct letter in box 13 on your answer sheet.

What is the writer's overall purpose in writing this article?

   A   to compare different methods of dealing with auditory problems
   B   to provide solutions for overly noisy learning environments
   C   to increase awareness of the situation of children with auditory problems
   D   to promote New Zealand as a model for other countries to follow

READING PASSAGE 2

*You should spend about 20 minutes on **Questions 14–26**, which are based on Reading Passage 2 below.*

Venus in transit

June 2004 saw the first passage, known as a 'transit', of the planet Venus across the face of the Sun in 122 years. Transits have helped shape our view of the whole Universe, as Heather Cooper and Nigel Henbest explain

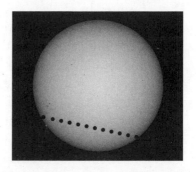

A On 8 June 2004, more than half the population of the world were treated to a rare astronomical event. For over six hours, the planet Venus steadily inched its way over the surface of the Sun. This 'transit' of Venus was the first since 6 December 1882. On that occasion, the American astronomer Professor Simon Newcomb led a party to South Africa to observe the event. They were based at a girls' school, where – it is alleged – the combined forces of three schoolmistresses outperformed the professionals with the accuracy of their observations.

B For centuries, transits of Venus have drawn explorers and astronomers alike to the four corners of the globe. And you can put it all down to the extraordinary polymath Edmond Halley. In November 1677, Halley observed a transit of the innermost planet, Mercury, from the desolate island of St Helena in the South Pacific. He realised that, from different latitudes, the passage of the planet across the Sun's disc would appear to differ. By timing the transit from two widely-separated locations, teams of astronomers could calculate the parallax angle – the apparent difference in position of an astronomical body due to a difference in the observer's position. Calculating this angle would allow astronomers to measure what was then the ultimate goal: the distance of the Earth from the Sun. This distance is known as the 'astronomical unit' or AU.

C Halley was aware that the AU was one of the most fundamental of all astronomical measurements. Johannes Kepler, in the early 17th century, had shown that the distances of the planets from the Sun governed their orbital speeds, which were easily measurable. But no-one had found a way to calculate accurate distances to the planets from the Earth. The goal was to measure the AU; then, knowing the orbital speeds of all the other planets round the Sun, the scale of the Solar System would fall into place. However, Halley realised that Mercury was so far away that its parallax angle would be very difficult to determine. As Venus was closer to the Earth, its parallax angle would be larger, and Halley worked out that by using Venus it would be possible to measure the

Sun's distance to 1 part in 500. But there was a problem: transits of Venus, unlike those of Mercury, are rare, occurring in pairs roughly eight years apart every hundred or so years. Nevertheless, he accurately predicted that Venus would cross the face of the Sun in both 1761 and 1769 – though he didn't survive to see either.

D   Inspired by Halley's suggestion of a way to pin down the scale of the Solar System, teams of British and French astronomers set out on expeditions to places as diverse as India and Siberia. But things weren't helped by Britain and France being at war. The person who deserves most sympathy is the French astronomer Guillaume Le Gentil. He was thwarted by the fact that the British were besieging his observation site at Pondicherry in India. Fleeing on a French warship crossing the Indian Ocean, Le Gentil saw a wonderful transit – but the ship's pitching and rolling ruled out any attempt at making accurate observations. Undaunted, he remained south of the equator, keeping himself busy by studying the islands of Mauritius and Madagascar before setting off to observe the next transit in the Philippines. Ironically after travelling nearly 50,000 kilometres, his view was clouded out at the last moment, a very dispiriting experience.

E   While the early transit timings were as precise as instruments would allow, the measurements were dogged by the 'black drop' effect. When Venus begins to cross the Sun's disc, it looks smeared not circular – which makes it difficult to establish timings. This is due to diffraction of light. The second problem is that Venus exhibits a halo of light when it is seen just outside the Sun's disc. While this showed astronomers that Venus was surrounded by a thick layer of gases refracting sunlight around it, both effects made it impossible to obtain accurate timings.

F   But astronomers laboured hard to analyse the results of these expeditions to observe Venus transits. Johann Franz Encke, Director of the Berlin Observatory, finally determined a value for the AU based on all these parallax measurements: 153,340,000 km. Reasonably accurate for the time, that is quite close to today's value of 149,597,870 km, determined by radar, which has now superseded transits and all other methods in accuracy. The AU is a cosmic measuring rod, and the basis of how we scale the Universe today. The parallax principle can be extended to measure the distances to the stars. If we look at a star in January – when Earth is at one point in its orbit – it will seem to be in a different position from where it appears six months later. Knowing the width of Earth's orbit, the parallax shift lets astronomers calculate the distance.

G   June 2004's transit of Venus was thus more of an astronomical spectacle than a scientifically important event. But such transits have paved the way for what might prove to be one of the most vital breakthroughs in the cosmos – detecting Earth-sized planets orbiting other stars.

Questions 14–17

Reading Passage 2 has seven paragraphs, **A–G**.

Which paragraph contains the following information?

*Write the correct letter, **A–G**, in boxes 14–17 on your answer sheet.*

14 examples of different ways in which the parallax principle has been applied

15 a description of an event which prevented a transit observation

16 a statement about potential future discoveries leading on from transit observations

17 a description of physical states connected with Venus which early astronomical instruments failed to overcome

Questions 18–21

Look at the following statements (Questions 18–21) and the list of people below.

*Match each statement with the correct person, **A**, **B**, **C** or **D**.*

*Write the correct letter, **A**, **B**, **C** or **D**, in boxes 18–21 on your answer sheet.*

18 He calculated the distance of the Sun from the Earth based on observations of Venus with a fair degree of accuracy.

19 He understood that the distance of the Sun from the Earth could be worked out by comparing observations of a transit.

20 He realised that the time taken by a planet to go round the Sun depends on its distance from the Sun.

21 He witnessed a Venus transit but was unable to make any calculations.

List of People
A Edmond Halley
B Johannes Kepler
C Guillaume Le Gentil
D Johann Franz Encke

Questions 22–26

Do the following statements agree with the information given in Reading Passage 2?

In boxes 22–26 on your answer sheet, write

> **TRUE**   *if the statement agrees with the information*
> **FALSE**   *if the statement contradicts the information*
> **NOT GIVEN**   *if there is no information on this*

22   Halley observed one transit of the planet Venus.

23   Le Gentil managed to observe a second Venus transit.

24   The shape of Venus appears distorted when it starts to pass in front of the Sun.

25   Early astronomers suspected that the atmosphere on Venus was toxic.

26   The parallax principle allows astronomers to work out how far away distant stars are from the Earth.

READING PASSAGE 3

*You should spend about 20 minutes on **Questions 27–40**, which are based on Reading Passage 3 below.*

A neuroscientist reveals how to think differently

In the last decade a revolution has occurred in the way that scientists think about the brain. We now know that the decisions humans make can be traced to the firing patterns of neurons in specific parts of the brain. These discoveries have led to the field known as *neuroeconomics*, which studies the brain's secrets to success in an economic environment that demands innovation and being able to do things differently from competitors. A brain that can do this is an iconoclastic one. Briefly, an *iconoclast* is a person who does something that others say can't be done.

This definition implies that iconoclasts are different from other people, but more precisely, it is their brains that are different in three distinct ways: perception, fear response, and social intelligence. Each of these three functions utilizes a different circuit in the brain. Naysayers might suggest that the brain is irrelevant, that thinking in an original, even revolutionary, way is more a matter of personality than brain function. But the field of neuroeconomics was born out of the realization that the physical workings of the brain place limitations on the way we make decisions. By understanding these constraints, we begin to understand why some people march to a different drumbeat.

The first thing to realize is that the brain suffers from limited resources. It has a fixed energy budget, about the same as a 40 watt light bulb, so it has evolved to work as efficiently as possible. This is where most people are impeded from being an iconoclast. For example, when confronted with information streaming from the eyes, the brain will interpret this information in the quickest way possible. Thus it will draw on both past experience and any other source of information, such as what other people say, to make sense of what it is seeing. This happens all the time. The brain takes shortcuts that work so well we are hardly ever aware of them. We think our perceptions of the world are real, but they are only biological and electrical rumblings. Perception is not simply a product of what your eyes or ears transmit to your brain. More than the physical reality of photons or sound waves, perception is a product of the brain.

Perception is central to iconoclasm. Iconoclasts see things differently to other people. Their brains do not fall into efficiency pitfalls as much as the average person's brain. Iconoclasts, either because they were born that way or through learning, have found ways to work around the perceptual shortcuts that plague most people. Perception is not something that is hardwired into the brain. It is a learned process, which is both a curse and an opportunity for change. The brain faces the fundamental problem of interpreting physical stimuli from the senses. Everything the brain sees, hears, or touches has multiple interpretations. The one that is ultimately chosen is simply the brain's best theory. In technical terms, these conjectures have their basis in the statistical likelihood of one interpretation over another and are heavily influenced by past experience and, importantly for potential iconoclasts, what other people say.

The best way to see things differently to other people is to bombard the brain with things it has never encountered before. Novelty releases the perceptual process from the chains of past experience and forces the brain to make new judgments. Successful iconoclasts have an extraordinary willingness to be exposed to what is fresh and different. Observation of iconoclasts shows that they embrace novelty while most people avoid things that are different.

The problem with novelty, however, is that it tends to trigger the brain's fear system. Fear is a major impediment to thinking like an iconoclast and stops the average person in his tracks. There are many types of fear, but the two that inhibit iconoclastic thinking and people generally find difficult to deal with are *fear of uncertainty* and *fear of public ridicule*. These may seem like trivial phobias. But fear of public speaking, which everyone must do from time to time, afflicts one-third of the population. This makes it too common to be considered a mental disorder. It is simply a common variant of human nature, one which iconoclasts do not let inhibit their reactions.

Finally, to be successful iconoclasts, individuals must sell their ideas to other people. This is where *social intelligence* comes in. Social intelligence is the ability to understand and manage people in a business setting. In the last decade there has been an explosion of knowledge about the social brain and how the brain works when groups coordinate decision making. Neuroscience has revealed which brain circuits are responsible for functions like understanding what other people think, empathy, fairness, and social identity. These brain regions play key roles in whether people convince others of their ideas. Perception is important in social cognition too. The perception of someone's enthusiasm, or reputation, can make or break a deal. Understanding how perception becomes intertwined with social decision making shows why successful iconoclasts are so rare.

Iconoclasts create new opportunities in every area from artistic expression to technology to business. They supply creativity and innovation not easily accomplished by committees. Rules aren't important to them. Iconoclasts face alienation and failure, but can also be a major asset to any organization. It is crucial for success in any field to understand how the iconoclastic mind works.

Questions 27–31

*Choose the correct letter, **A**, **B**, **C** or **D**.*

Write the correct letter in boxes 27–31 on your answer sheet.

27   Neuroeconomics is a field of study which seeks to

   A   cause a change in how scientists understand brain chemistry.
   B   understand how good decisions are made in the brain.
   C   understand how the brain is linked to achievement in competitive fields.
   D   trace the specific firing patterns of neurons in different areas of the brain.

28   According to the writer, iconoclasts are distinctive because

   A   they create unusual brain circuits.
   B   their brains function differently.
   C   their personalities are distinctive.
   D   they make decisions easily.

29   According to the writer, the brain works efficiently because

   A   it uses the eyes quickly.
   B   it interprets data logically.
   C   it generates its own energy.
   D   it relies on previous events.

30   The writer says that perception is

   A   a combination of photons and sound waves.
   B   a reliable product of what your senses transmit.
   C   a result of brain processes.
   D   a process we are usually conscious of.

31   According to the writer, an iconoclastic thinker

   A   centralises perceptual thinking in one part of the brain.
   B   avoids cognitive traps.
   C   has a brain that is hardwired for learning.
   D   has more opportunities than the average person.

Questions 32–37

Do the following statements agree with the claims of the writer in Reading Passage 3?

In boxes 32–37 on your answer sheet, write

> **YES**   if the statement agrees with the claims of the writer
> **NO**   if the statement contradicts the claims of the writer
> **NOT GIVEN**   if it is impossible to say what the writer thinks about this

32 Exposure to different events forces the brain to think differently.

33 Iconoclasts are unusually receptive to new experiences.

34 Most people are too shy to try different things.

35 If you think in an iconoclastic way, you can easily overcome fear.

36 When concern about embarrassment matters less, other fears become irrelevant.

37 Fear of public speaking is a psychological illness.

Questions 38–40

*Complete each sentence with the correct ending, **A–E**, below.*

*Write the correct letter, **A–E**, in boxes 38–40 on your answer sheet.*

38 Thinking like a successful iconoclast is demanding because it

39 The concept of the social brain is useful to iconoclasts because it

40 Iconoclasts are generally an asset because their way of thinking

> **A** requires both perceptual and social intelligence skills.
> **B** focuses on how groups decide on an action.
> **C** works in many fields, both artistic and scientific.
> **D** leaves one open to criticism and rejection.
> **E** involves understanding how organisations manage people.

WRITING

WRITING TASK 1

You should spend about 20 minutes on this task.

> *The chart below shows the total number of minutes (in billions) of telephone calls in the UK, divided into three categories, from 1995–2002.*
>
> *Summarise the information by selecting and reporting the main features, and make comparisons where relevant.*

Write at least 150 words.

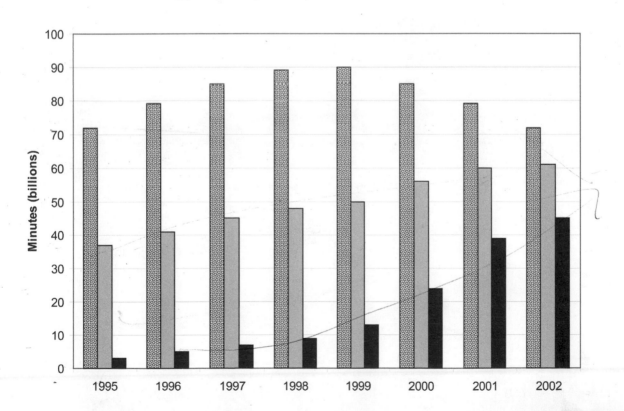

UK telephone calls, by category, 1995–2002

Call type:
- Local – fixed line
- National and international – fixed line
- Mobiles (all calls)

WRITING TASK 2

You should spend about 40 minutes on this task.

Write about the following topic:

> *Some people believe that unpaid community service should be a compulsory part of high school programmes (for example working for a charity, improving the neighbourhood or teaching sports to younger children).*
>
> *To what extent do you agree or disagree?*

Give reasons for your answer and include any relevant examples from your own knowledge or experience.

Write at least 250 words.

SPEAKING

PART 1

The examiner asks the candidate about him/herself, his/her home, work or studies and other familiar topics.

EXAMPLE

Giving gifts

- When do people give gifts or presents in your country?
- Do you ever take a gift when you visit someone in their home? [Why/Why not?]
- When did you last receive a gift? [What was it?]
- Do you enjoy looking for gifts for people? [Why/Why not?]

PART 2

Describe something you did that was new or exciting.

You should say:
    what you did
    where and when you did this
    who you shared the activity with
and explain why this activity was new or exciting for you.

You will have to talk about the topic for one to two minutes.
You have one minute to think about what you are going to say.
You can make some notes to help you if you wish.

PART 3

Discussion topics:

Doing new things

Example questions:
Why do you think some people like doing new things?
What problems can people have when they try new activities for the first time?
Do you think it's best to do new things on your own or with other people? Why?

Learning new things

Example questions:
What kinds of things do children learn to do when they are very young? How important are these things?
Do you think children and adults learn to do new things in the same way? How is their learning style different?
Some people say that it is more important to be able to learn new things now than it was in the past. Do you agree or disagree with that? Why?

Test 3

LISTENING

SECTION 1   Questions 1–10

Questions 1–5

Complete the table below.

Write **ONE WORD AND/OR A NUMBER** for each answer.

Apartments	Facilities	Other Information	Cost
Rose Garden Apartments	studio flat	*Example* entertainment programme: Greek ....dancing....	£219
Blue Bay Apartments	large salt-water swimming pool	- just **1** .... metres from beach - near shops	£275
2 .... **Apartments**	terrace	watersports	£490
The Grand	- Greek paintings - **3**	- overlooking **4** .... - near a supermarket and a disco	**5** £ ....

Questions 6–10

Complete the table below.

Write ONE WORD AND/OR A NUMBER for each answer.

GREEK ISLAND HOLIDAYS	
Insurance Benefits	**Maximum Amount**
Cancellation	**6** £ ....
Hospital	£600. Additional benefit allows a **7** .... to travel to resort
8 .... departure	Up to £1000. Depends on reason
Personal belongings	Up to £3000; £500 for one **9** ....
Name of Assistant Manager: Ben **10**	
Direct phone line: 081260 543216	

SECTION 2   *Questions 11–20*

Questions 11–13

Choose the correct letter, A, B or C.

Winridge Forest Railway Park

11   Simon's idea for a theme park came from

    A   his childhood hobby.
    B   his interest in landscape design.
    C   his visit to another park.

12   When they started, the family decided to open the park only when

    A   the weather was expected to be good.
    B   the children weren't at school.
    C   there were fewer farming commitments.

13   Since opening, the park has had

    A   50,000 visitors.
    B   1,000,000 visitors.
    C   1,500,000 visitors.

Questions 14–18

What is currently the main area of work of each of the following people?

Choose FIVE answers from the box and write the correct letter, A–H, next to questions 14–18.

Area of work
A   advertising
B   animal care
C   building
D   educational links
E   engine maintenance
F   food and drink
G   sales
H   staffing

People

14   Simon (the speaker)   ....

15   Liz   ....

16   Sarah   ....

17   Duncan   ....

18   Judith   ....

Questions 19 and 20

Complete the table below.

Write **ONE WORD AND/OR NUMBERS** for each answer.

Feature	Size	Biggest challenge	Target age group
Railway	1.2 km	Making tunnels	
Go-Kart arena	19 .... m^2	Removing mounds on the track	20 .... year-olds

SECTION 3   *Questions 21–30*

Complete the notes below.

*Write **NO MORE THAN TWO WORDS AND/OR A NUMBER** for each answer.*

Study Skills Tutorial – Caroline Benning

Dissertation topic: the **21** ....

Strengths: • **22** ....

                     • computer modelling

Weaknesses: • lack of background information

                     • poor **23** .... skills

Possible strategy	Benefits	Problems
peer group discussion	increases **24**	dissertations tend to contain the same **25** ....
use the **26** .... service	provides structured programme	limited **27** ....
consult study skills books	are a good source of reference	can be too **28** ....

Recommendations: • use a card index

                     • read all notes **29** ....

Next tutorial date: **30** .... January

SECTION 4   *Questions 31–40*

Questions 31 and 32

Choose the correct letter, A, B or C.

31   The owners of the underground house

    A   had no experience of living in a rural area.
    B   were interested in environmental issues.
    C   wanted a professional project manager.

32   What does the speaker say about the site of the house?

    A   The land was quite cheap.
    B   Stone was being extracted nearby.
    C   It was in a completely unspoilt area.

Test 3

Questions 33–40

Complete the notes below.

Write **ONE WORD AND/OR A NUMBER** for each answer.

The Underground House

Design

- Built in the earth, with two floors
- The south-facing side was constructed of two layers of **33** ....
- Photovoltaic tiles were attached
- A layer of foam was used to improve the **34** .... of the building

Special features

- To increase the light, the building has many internal mirrors and **35** ....
- In future, the house may produce more **36** .... than it needs
- Recycled wood was used for the **37** .... of the house
- The system for processing domestic **38** .... is organic

Environmental issues

- The use of large quantities of **39** .... in construction was environmentally harmful
- But the house will have paid its 'environmental debt' within **40** ....

READING PASSAGE 1

*You should spend about 20 minutes on **Questions 1–13**, which are based on Reading Passage 1 below.*

Attitudes to language

It is not easy to be systematic and objective about language study. Popular linguistic debate regularly deteriorates into invective and polemic. Language belongs to everyone, so most people feel they have a right to hold an opinion about it. And when opinions differ, emotions can run high. Arguments can start as easily over minor points of usage as over major policies of linguistic education.

Language, moreover, is a very public behaviour, so it is easy for different usages to be noted and criticised. No part of society or social behaviour is exempt: linguistic factors influence how we judge personality, intelligence, social status, educational standards, job aptitude, and many other areas of identity and social survival. As a result, it is easy to hurt, and to be hurt, when language use is unfeelingly attacked.

In its most general sense, prescriptivism is the view that one variety of language has an inherently higher value than others, and that this ought to be imposed on the whole of the speech community. The view is propounded especially in relation to grammar and vocabulary, and frequently with reference to pronunciation. The variety which is favoured, in this account, is usually a version of the 'standard' written language, especially as encountered in literature, or in the formal spoken language which most closely reflects this style. Adherents to this variety are said to speak or write 'correctly'; deviations from it are said to be 'incorrect'.

All the main languages have been studied prescriptively, especially in the 18th century approach to the writing of grammars and dictionaries. The aims of these early grammarians were threefold: (a) they wanted to codify the principles of their languages, to show that there was a system beneath the apparent chaos of usage, (b) they wanted a means of settling disputes over usage, and (c) they wanted to point out what they felt to be common errors, in order to 'improve' the language. The authoritarian nature of the approach is best characterised by its reliance on 'rules' of grammar. Some usages are 'prescribed', to be learnt and followed accurately; others are 'proscribed', to be avoided. In this early period, there were no half-measures: usage was either right or wrong, and it was the task of the grammarian not simply to record alternatives, but to pronounce judgement upon them.

These attitudes are still with us, and they motivate a widespread concern that linguistic standards should be maintained. Nevertheless, there is an alternative point of view that is concerned less with standards than with the *facts* of linguistic usage. This approach is summarised in the statement that it is the task of the grammarian to *describe*, not *prescribe*

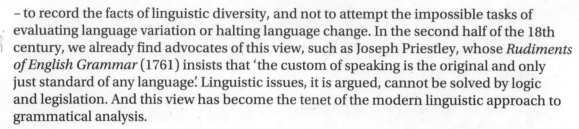

– to record the facts of linguistic diversity, and not to attempt the impossible tasks of evaluating language variation or halting language change. In the second half of the 18th century, we already find advocates of this view, such as Joseph Priestley, whose *Rudiments of English Grammar* (1761) insists that 'the custom of speaking is the original and only just standard of any language'. Linguistic issues, it is argued, cannot be solved by logic and legislation. And this view has become the tenet of the modern linguistic approach to grammatical analysis.

In our own time, the opposition between 'descriptivists' and 'prescriptivists' has often become extreme, with both sides painting unreal pictures of the other. Descriptive grammarians have been presented as people who do not care about standards, because of the way they see all forms of usage as equally valid. Prescriptive grammarians have been presented as blind adherents to a historical tradition. The opposition has even been presented in quasi-political terms – of radical liberalism vs elitist conservatism.

Questions 1–8

Do the following statements agree with the claims of the writer in Reading Passage 1?

In boxes 1–8 on your answer sheet, write

YES	*if the statement agrees with the claims of the writer*
NO	*if the statement contradicts the claims of the writer*
NOT GIVEN	*if it is impossible to say what the writer thinks about this*

1   There are understandable reasons why arguments occur about language.

2   People feel more strongly about language education than about small differences in language usage.

3   Our assessment of a person's intelligence is affected by the way he or she uses language.

4   Prescriptive grammar books cost a lot of money to buy in the 18th century.

5   Prescriptivism still exists today.

6   According to descriptivists it is pointless to try to stop language change.

7   Descriptivism only appeared after the 18th century.

8   Both descriptivists and prescriptivists have been misrepresented.

Questions 9–12

Complete the summary using the list of words, A–I, below.

Write the correct letter, A–I, in boxes 9–12 on your answer sheet.

The language debate

According to **9** .... , there is only one correct form of language. Linguists who take this approach to language place great importance on grammatical **10** .... Conversely, the view of **11** .... , such as Joseph Priestley, is that grammar should be based on **12** ....

A	descriptivists	**B**	language experts	**C**	popular speech
D	formal language	**E**	evaluation	**F**	rules
G	modern linguists	**H**	prescriptivists	**I**	change

Question 13

Choose the correct letter, A, B, C or D.

Write the correct letter in box 13 on your answer sheet.

What is the writer's purpose in Reading Passage 1?

    A   to argue in favour of a particular approach to writing dictionaries and grammar books
    B   to present a historical account of differing views of language
    C   to describe the differences between spoken and written language
    D   to show how a certain view of language has been discredited

READING PASSAGE 2

*You should spend about 20 minutes on **Questions 14–26**, which are based on Reading Passage 2 below.*

Tidal Power

Undersea turbines which produce electricity from the tides are set to become an important source of renewable energy for Britain. It is still too early to predict the extent of the impact they may have, but all the signs are that they will play a significant role in the future

A   Operating on the same principle as wind turbines, the power in sea turbines comes from tidal currents which turn blades similar to ships' propellers, but, unlike wind, the tides are predictable and the power input is constant. The technology raises the prospect of Britain becoming self-sufficient in renewable energy and drastically reducing its carbon dioxide emissions. If tide, wind and wave power are all developed, Britain would be able to close gas, coal and nuclear power plants and export renewable power to other parts of Europe. Unlike wind power, which Britain originally developed and then abandoned for 20 years allowing the Dutch to make it a major industry, undersea turbines could become a big export earner to island nations such as Japan and New Zealand.

B   Tidal sites have already been identified that will produce one sixth or more of the UK's power – and at prices competitive with modern gas turbines and undercutting those of the already ailing nuclear industry. One site alone, the Pentland Firth, between Orkney and mainland Scotland, could produce 10% of the country's electricity with banks of turbines under the sea, and another at Alderney in the Channel Islands three times the 1,200 megawatts of Britain's largest and newest nuclear plant, Sizewell B, in Suffolk. Other sites identified include the Bristol Channel and the west coast of Scotland, particularly the channel between Campbeltown and Northern Ireland.

C   Work on designs for the new turbine blades and sites are well advanced at the University of Southampton's sustainable energy research group. The first station is expected to be installed off Lynmouth in Devon shortly to test the technology in a venture jointly funded by the department of Trade and Industry and the European Union. AbuBakr Bahaj, in charge of the Southampton research, said: 'The prospects for energy from tidal currents are far better than from wind because the flows of water are predictable and constant. The technology for dealing with the hostile saline environment under the sea has been developed in the North Sea oil industry and much is already known about turbine blade design, because of wind power and ship propellers. There are a few technical difficulties, but I believe in the next five to ten years we will be installing commercial marine turbine farms.' Southampton has been awarded £215,000 over three years to develop the turbines and is working with Marine Current Turbines, a subsidiary of IT power, on the Lynmouth project. EU research has now identified 106 potential sites for tidal power, 80% round the coasts of Britain. The best sites are between islands or around heavily indented coasts where there are strong tidal currents.

D   A marine turbine blade needs to be only one third of the size of a wind generator to produce three times as much power. The blades will be about 20 metres in diameter, so around 30 metres of water is required. Unlike wind power, there are unlikely to be environmental objections. Fish and other creatures are thought unlikely to be at risk from the relatively slow-turning blades. Each turbine will be mounted on a tower which will connect to the national power supply grid via underwater cables. The towers will stick out of the water and be lit, to warn shipping, and also be designed to be lifted out of the water for maintenance and to clean seaweed from the blades.

E   Dr Bahaj has done most work on the Alderney site, where there are powerful currents. The single undersea turbine farm would produce far more power than needed for the Channel Islands and most would be fed into the French Grid and be re-imported into Britain via the cable under the Channel.

F   One technical difficulty is cavitation, where low pressure behind a turning blade causes air bubbles. These can cause vibration and damage the blades of the turbines. Dr Bahaj said: 'We have to test a number of blade types to avoid this happening or at least make sure it does not damage the turbines or reduce performance. Another slight concern is submerged debris floating into the blades. So far we do not know how much of a problem it might be. We will have to make the turbines robust because the sea is a hostile environment, but all the signs that we can do it are good.'

Questions 14–17

Reading Passage 2 has six paragraphs, **A–F**.

Which paragraph contains the following information?

*Write the correct letter, **A–F**, in boxes 14–17 on your answer sheet.*

***NB** You may use any letter more than once.*

14 the location of the first test site

15 a way of bringing the power produced on one site back into Britain

16 a reference to a previous attempt by Britain to find an alternative source of energy

17 mention of the possibility of applying technology from another industry

Questions 18–22

Choose **FIVE** letters, **A–J**.

Write the correct letters in boxes 18–22 on your answer sheet.

Which **FIVE** of the following claims about tidal power are made by the writer?

A	It is a more reliable source of energy than wind power.
B	It would replace all other forms of energy in Britain.
C	Its introduction has come as a result of public pressure.
D	It would cut down on air pollution.
E	It could contribute to the closure of many existing power stations in Britain.
F	It could be a means of increasing national income.
G	It could face a lot of resistance from other fuel industries.
H	It could be sold more cheaply than any other type of fuel.
I	It could compensate for the shortage of inland sites for energy production.
J	It is best produced in the vicinity of coastlines with particular features.

Questions 23–26

Label the diagram below.

*Choose **NO MORE THAN TWO WORDS** from the passage for each answer.*

Write your answers in boxes 23–26 on your answer sheet.

An Undersea Turbine

Whole tower can be raised
for **23** .... and the extraction
of seaweed from the blades

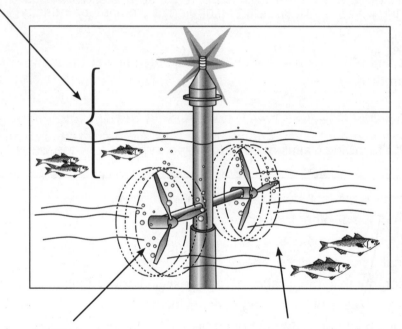

Air bubbles result from
the **25** .... behind blades.
This is known as **26** ....

Sea life not in danger due to the
fact that blades are comparatively
24 ....

READING PASSAGE 3

*You should spend about 20 minutes on **Questions 27–40**, which are based on Reading Passage 3 below.*

Information theory – the big idea

Information theory lies at the heart of everything – from DVD players and the genetic code of DNA to the physics of the universe at its most fundamental. It has been central to the development of the science of communication, which enables data to be sent electronically and has therefore had a major impact on our lives

A In April 2002 an event took place which demonstrated one of the many applications of information theory. The space probe, Voyager I, launched in 1977, had sent back spectacular images of Jupiter and Saturn and then soared out of the Solar System on a one-way mission to the stars. After 25 years of exposure to the freezing temperatures of deep space, the probe was beginning to show its age. Sensors and circuits were on the brink of failing and NASA experts realised that they had to do something or lose contact with their probe forever. The solution was to get a message to Voyager I to instruct it to use spares to change the failing parts. With the probe 12 billion kilometres from Earth, this was not an easy task. By means of a radio dish belonging to NASA's Deep Space Network, the message was sent out into the depths of space. Even travelling at the speed of light, it took over 11 hours to reach its target, far beyond the orbit of Pluto. Yet, incredibly, the little probe managed to hear the faint call from its home planet, and successfully made the switchover.

B It was the longest-distance repair job in history, and a triumph for the NASA engineers. But it also highlighted the astonishing power of the techniques developed by American communications engineer Claude Shannon, who had died just a year earlier. Born in 1916 in Petoskey, Michigan, Shannon showed an early talent for maths and for building gadgets, and made breakthroughs in the foundations of computer technology when still a student. While at Bell Laboratories, Shannon developed information theory, but shunned the resulting acclaim. In the 1940s, he single-handedly created an entire science of communication which has since inveigled its way into a host of applications, from DVDs to satellite communications to bar codes – any area, in short, where data has to be conveyed rapidly yet accurately.

71

C This all seems light years away from the down-to-earth uses Shannon originally had for his work, which began when he was a 22-year-old graduate engineering student at the prestigious Massachusetts Institute of Technology in 1939. He set out with an apparently simple aim: to pin down the precise meaning of the concept of 'information'. The most basic form of information, Shannon argued, is whether something is true or false – which can be captured in the binary unit, or 'bit', of the form 1 or 0. Having identified this fundamental unit, Shannon set about defining otherwise vague ideas about information and how to transmit it from place to place. In the process he discovered something surprising: it is always possible to guarantee information will get through random interference – 'noise' – intact.

D Noise usually means unwanted sounds which interfere with genuine information. Information theory generalises this idea via theorems that capture the effects of noise with mathematical precision. In particular, Shannon showed that noise sets a limit on the rate at which information can pass along communication channels while remaining error-free. This rate depends on the relative strengths of the signal and noise travelling down the communication channel, and on its capacity (its 'bandwidth'). The resulting limit, given in units of bits per second, is the absolute maximum rate of error-free communication given signal strength and noise level. The trick, Shannon showed, is to find ways of packaging up – 'coding' – information to cope with the ravages of noise, while staying within the information-carrying capacity – 'bandwidth' – of the communication system being used.

E Over the years scientists have devised many such coding methods, and they have proved crucial in many technological feats. The Voyager spacecraft transmitted data using codes which added one extra bit for every single bit of information; the result was an error rate of just one bit in 10,000 – and stunningly clear pictures of the planets. Other codes have become part of everyday life – such as the Universal Product Code, or bar code, which uses a simple error-detecting system that ensures supermarket check-out lasers can read the price even on, say, a crumpled bag of crisps. As recently as 1993, engineers made a major breakthrough by discovering so-called turbo codes – which come very close to Shannon's ultimate limit for the maximum rate that data can be transmitted reliably, and now play a key role in the mobile videophone revolution.

F Shannon also laid the foundations of more efficient ways of storing information, by stripping out superfluous ('redundant') bits from data which contributed little real information. As mobile phone text messages like 'I CN C U' show, it is often possible to leave out a lot of data without losing much meaning. As with error correction, however, there's a limit beyond which messages become too ambiguous. Shannon showed how to calculate this limit, opening the way to the design of compression methods that cram maximum information into the minimum space.

Questions 27–32

Reading Passage 3 has six paragraphs, **A–F**.

Which paragraph contains the following information?

*Write the correct letter, **A–F**, in boxes 27–32 on your answer sheet.*

27   an explanation of the factors affecting the transmission of information

28   an example of how unnecessary information can be omitted

29   a reference to Shannon's attitude to fame

30   details of a machine capable of interpreting incomplete information

31   a detailed account of an incident involving information theory

32   a reference to what Shannon initially intended to achieve in his research

Questions 33–37

Complete the notes below.

Choose **NO MORE THAN TWO WORDS** from the passage for each answer.

Write your answers in boxes 33–37 on your answer sheet.

The Voyager 1 Space Probe

- The probe transmitted pictures of both 33 .... and .... , then left the 34 ....

- The freezing temperatures were found to have a negative effect on parts of the space probe.

- Scientists feared that both the 35 .... and .... were about to stop working.

- The only hope was to tell the probe to replace them with 36 .... – but distance made communication with the probe difficult.

- A 37 .... was used to transmit the message at the speed of light.

- The message was picked up by the probe and the switchover took place.

Questions 38–40

Do the following statements agree with the information given in Reading Passage 3?

In boxes 38–40 on your answer sheet, write

TRUE	*if the statement agrees with the information*
FALSE	*if the statement contradicts the information*
NOT GIVEN	*if there is no information on this*

38   The concept of describing something as true or false was the starting point for Shannon in his attempts to send messages over distances.

39   The amount of information that can be sent in a given time period is determined with reference to the signal strength and noise level.

40   Products have now been developed which can convey more information than Shannon had anticipated as possible.

WRITING

WRITING TASK 1

You should spend about 20 minutes on this task.

> ***The charts below give information on the ages of the populations of Yemen and Italy in 2000 and projections for 2050.***
>
> ***Summarise the information by selecting and reporting the main features, and make comparisons where relevant.***

Write at least 150 words.

YEMEN

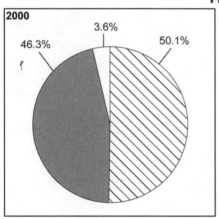

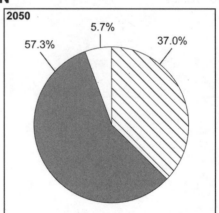

ITALY

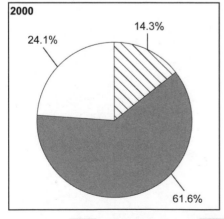

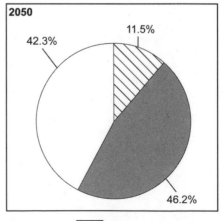

0–14 years   15–59 years   60+ years

WRITING TASK 2

You should spend about 40 minutes on this task.

Write about the following topic:

> *Some people say that the best way to improve public health is by increasing the number of sports facilities. Others, however, say that this would have little effect on public health and that other measures are required.*
>
> *Discuss both these views and give your own opinion.*

Give reasons for your answer and include any relevant examples from your own knowledge or experience.

Write at least 250 words.

SPEAKING

PART 1

The examiner asks the candidate about him/herself, his/her home, work or studies and other familiar topics.

EXAMPLE

Telephoning

- How often do you make telephone calls? [Why/Why not?]
- Who do you spend most time talking to on the telephone? [Why?]
- When do you think you'll next make a telephone call? [Why?]
- Do you sometimes prefer to send a text message instead of telephoning? [Why/Why not?]

PART 2

Describe a journey [e.g. by car, plane, boat] that you remember well.

You should say:
> **where you went**
> **how you travelled**
> **why you went on the journey**
and explain why you remember this journey well.

You will have to talk about the topic for one to two minutes.
You have one minute to think about what you are going to say.
You can make some notes to help you if you wish.

PART 3

Discussion topics:

Reasons for daily travel

Example questions:
Why do people need to travel every day?
What problems can people have when they are on their daily journey, for example to work or school? Why is this?
Some people say that daily journeys like these will not be so common in the future. Do you agree or disagree? Why?

Benefits of international travel

Example questions:
What do you think people can learn from travelling to other countries? Why?
Can travel make a positive difference to the economy of a country? How?
Do you think a society can benefit if its members have experience of travelling to other countries? In what ways?

Test 4

SECTION 1   *Questions 1–10*

Questions 1–4

Complete the table below.

*Write **ONE WORD ONLY** for each answer.*

Health Centres		
Name of centre	**Doctor's name**	**Advantage**
The Harvey Clinic	*Example* Dr ....*Green*....	especially good with **1** ....
The **2** .... Health Practice	Dr Fuller	offers **3** .... appointments
The Shore Lane Health Centre	Dr **4**	

Questions 5–6

*Choose **TWO** letters, **A–E**.*

Which **TWO** of the following are offered free of charge at Shore Lane Health Centre?
- **A**   acupuncture
- **B**   employment medicals
- **C**   sports injury therapy
- **D**   travel advice
- **E**   vaccinations

Questions 7–10

Complete the table below.

Write **NO MORE THAN TWO WORDS AND/OR A NUMBER** *for each answer.*

Talks for patients at Shore Lane Health Centre			
Subject of talk	**Date/Time**	**Location**	**Notes**
Giving up smoking	25th February at 7pm	room 4	useful for people with asthma or **7** .... problems
Healthy eating	1st March at 5pm	the **8** .... (Shore Lane)	anyone welcome
Avoiding injuries during exercise	9th March at **9**	room 6	for all **10** ....

SECTION 2   *Questions 11–20*

Questions 11–13

Label the diagram below.

*Choose **THREE** answers from the box and write the correct letter, **A–E**, next to questions 11–13.*

A	electricity indicator
B	on/off switch
C	reset button
D	time control
E	warning indicator

Water Heater

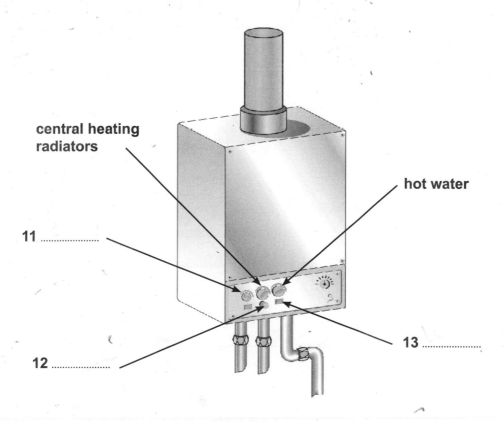

central heating radiators

hot water

11 ....

12 ....

13 ....

Questions 14–18

Where can each of the following items be found?

*Choose **FIVE** answers from the box and write the correct letter, **A–G**, next to questions 14–18.*

Locations
A in box on washing machine
B in cupboard on landing
C in chest of drawers
D next to window in living room
E on shelf by back door
F on top of television
G under kitchen sink

14 pillows ....

15 washing powder ....

16 key ....

17 light bulbs ....

18 map ....

Questions 19 and 20

Complete the notes below.

*Write **ONE WORD AND/OR A NUMBER** for each answer.*

The best place to park in town – next to the station
Phone number for takeaway pizzas – **19** ....
Railway museum closed on **20** ....

SECTION 3   *Questions 21–30*

Questions 21 and 22

*Choose the correct letter, **A**, **B** or **C**.*

21 In her home country, Kira had

    A completed a course.
    B done two years of a course.
    C found her course difficult.

22 To succeed with assignments, Kira had to

    A read faster.
    B write faster.
    C change her way of thinking.

Questions 23–25

Complete the sentences below.

*Write **ONE WORD ONLY** for each answer.*

23 Kira says that lecturers are easier to .... than those in her home country.

24 Paul suggests that Kira may be more .... than when she was studying before.

25 Kira says that students want to discuss things that worry them or that .... them very much.

Questions 26–30

Answer the questions below.

Write **NO MORE THAN THREE WORDS AND/OR A NUMBER** *for each answer.*

26   How did the students do their practical sessions?

....

27   In the second semester how often did Kira work in a hospital?

....

28   How much full-time work did Kira do during the year?

....

29   Having completed the year, how does Kira feel?

....

30   In addition to the language, what do overseas students need to become familiar
with?

....

SECTION 4   *Questions 31–40*

Questions 31–36

*Choose the correct letter, **A**, **B** or **C**.*

Wildlife in city gardens

31 What led the group to choose their topic?

   A   They were concerned about the decline of one species.
   B   They were interested in the effects of city growth.
   C   They wanted to investigate a recent phenomenon.

32 The exact proportion of land devoted to private gardens was confirmed by

   A   consulting some official documents.
   B   taking large-scale photos.
   C   discussions with town surveyors.

33 The group asked garden owners to

   A   take part in formal interviews.
   B   keep a record of animals they saw.
   C   get in contact when they saw a rare species.

34 The group made their observations in gardens

   A   which had a large number of animal species.
   B   which they considered to be representative.
   C   which had stable populations of rare animals.

35 The group did extensive reading on

   A   wildlife problems in rural areas.
   B   urban animal populations.
   C   current gardening practices.

36 The speaker focuses on three animal species because

   A   a lot of data has been obtained about them.
   B   the group were most interested in them.
   C   they best indicated general trends.

Questions 37–40

Complete the table below.

Write **ONE WORD ONLY** for each answer.

Animals	Reason for population increase in gardens	Comments
37	suitable stretches of water	massive increase in urban population
Hedgehogs	safer from **38** .... when in cities	easy to **39** .... them accurately
Song thrushes	– a variety of **40** .... to eat – more nesting places available	large survey starting soon

READING ✓

READING PASSAGE 1

*You should spend about 20 minutes on **Questions 1–13**, which are based on Reading Passage 1 below.*

The life and work of Marie Curie

Marie Curie is probably the most famous woman scientist who has ever lived. Born Maria Sklodowska in Poland in 1867, she is famous for her work on radioactivity, and was twice a winner of the Nobel Prize. With her husband, Pierre Curie, and Henri Becquerel, she was awarded the 1903 Nobel Prize for Physics, and was then sole winner of the 1911 Nobel Prize for Chemistry. She was the first woman to win a Nobel Prize.

From childhood, Marie was remarkable for her prodigious memory, and at the age of 16 won a gold medal on completion of her secondary education. Because her father lost his savings through bad investment, she then had to take work as a teacher. From her earnings she was able to finance her sister Bronia's medical studies in Paris, on the understanding that Bronia would, in turn, later help her to get an education.

In 1891 this promise was fulfilled and Marie went to Paris and began to study at the Sorbonne (the University of Paris). She often worked far into the night and lived on little more than bread and butter and tea. She came first in the examination in the physical sciences in 1893, and in 1894 was placed second in the examination in mathematical sciences. It was not until the spring of that year that she was introduced to Pierre Curie.

Their marriage in 1895 marked the start of a partnership that was soon to achieve results of world significance. Following Henri Becquerel's discovery in 1896 of a new phenomenon, which Marie later called 'radioactivity', Marie Curie decided to find out if the radioactivity discovered in uranium was to be found in other elements. She discovered that this was true for thorium.

Turning her attention to minerals, she found her interest drawn to pitchblende, a mineral whose radioactivity, superior to that of pure uranium, could be explained only by the presence in the ore of small quantities of an unknown substance of very high activity. Pierre Curie joined her in the work that she had undertaken to resolve this problem, and that led to the discovery of the new elements, polonium and radium. While Pierre Curie devoted himself chiefly to the physical study of the new radiations, Marie Curie struggled to obtain pure radium in the metallic state. This was achieved with the help of the chemist André-Louis Debierne, one of

Pierre Curie's pupils. Based on the results of this research, Marie Curie received her Doctorate of Science, and in 1903 Marie and Pierre shared with Becquerel the Nobel Prize for Physics for the discovery of radioactivity.

The births of Marie's two daughters, Irène and Eve, in 1897 and 1904 failed to interrupt her scientific work. She was appointed lecturer in physics at the École Normale Supérieure for girls in Sèvres, France (1900), and introduced a method of teaching based on experimental demonstrations. In December 1904 she was appointed chief assistant in the laboratory directed by Pierre Curie.

The sudden death of her husband in 1906 was a bitter blow to Marie Curie, but was also a turning point in her career: henceforth she was to devote all her energy to completing alone the scientific work that they had undertaken. On May 13, 1906, she was appointed to the professorship that had been left vacant on her husband's death, becoming the first woman to teach at the Sorbonne. In 1911 she was awarded the Nobel Prize for Chemistry for the isolation of a pure form of radium.

During World War I, Marie Curie, with the help of her daughter Irène, devoted herself to the development of the use of X-radiography, including the mobile units which came to be known as 'Little Curies', used for the treatment of wounded soldiers. In 1918 the Radium Institute, whose staff Irène had joined, began to operate in earnest, and became a centre for nuclear physics and chemistry. Marie Curie, now at the highest point of her fame and, from 1922, a member of the Academy of Medicine, researched the chemistry of radioactive substances and their medical applications.

In 1921, accompanied by her two daughters, Marie Curie made a triumphant journey to the United States to raise funds for research on radium. Women there presented her with a gram of radium for her campaign. Marie also gave lectures in Belgium, Brazil, Spain and Czechoslovakia and, in addition, had the satisfaction of seeing the development of the Curie Foundation in Paris, and the inauguration in 1932 in Warsaw of the Radium Institute, where her sister Bronia became director.

One of Marie Curie's outstanding achievements was to have understood the need to accumulate intense radioactive sources, not only to treat illness but also to maintain an abundant supply for research. The existence in Paris at the Radium Institute of a stock of 1.5 grams of radium made a decisive contribution to the success of the experiments undertaken in the years around 1930. This work prepared the way for the discovery of the neutron by Sir James Chadwick and, above all, for the discovery in 1934 by Irène and Frédéric Joliot-Curie of artificial radioactivity. A few months after this discovery, Marie Curie died as a result of leukaemia caused by exposure to radiation. She had often carried test tubes containing radioactive isotopes in her pocket, remarking on the pretty blue-green light they gave off.

Her contribution to physics had been immense, not only in her own work, the importance of which had been demonstrated by her two Nobel Prizes, but because of her influence on subsequent generations of nuclear physicists and chemists.

Questions 1–6

Do the following statements agree with the information given in Reading Passage 1?

In boxes 1–6 on your answer sheet, write

TRUE	*if the statement agrees with the information*
FALSE	*if the statement contradicts the information*
NOT GIVEN	*if there is no information on this*

1 Marie Curie's husband was a joint winner of both Marie's Nobel Prizes.

2 Marie became interested in science when she was a child.

3 Marie was able to attend the Sorbonne because of her sister's financial contribution.

4 Marie stopped doing research for several years when her children were born.

5 Marie took over the teaching position her husband had held.

6 Marie's sister Bronia studied the medical uses of radioactivity.

Test 4

Questions 7–13

Complete the notes below.

Choose **ONE WORD** from the passage for each answer.

Write your answers in boxes 7–13 on your answer sheet.

Marie Curie's research on radioactivity

- When uranium was discovered to be radioactive, Marie Curie found that the element called **7** .... had the same property.

- Marie and Pierre Curie's research into the radioactivity of the mineral known as **8** .... led to the discovery of two new elements.

- In 1911, Marie Curie received recognition for her work on the element **9** ....

- Marie and Irène Curie developed X-radiography which was used as a medical technique for **10** ....

- Marie Curie saw the importance of collecting radioactive material both for research and for cases of **11** ....

- The radioactive material stocked in Paris contributed to the discoveries in the 1930s of the **12** .... and of what was known as artificial radioactivity.

- During her research, Marie Curie was exposed to radiation and as a result she suffered from **13** ....

READING PASSAGE 2

*You should spend about 20 minutes on **Questions 14–26** which are based on Reading Passage 2 below.*

Young children's sense of identity

A   A sense of self develops in young children by degrees. The process can usefully be thought of in terms of the gradual emergence of two somewhat separate features: the *self as a subject*, and the *self as an object*. William James introduced the distinction in 1892, and contemporaries of his, such as Charles Cooley, added to the developing debate. Ever since then psychologists have continued building on the theory.

B   According to James, a child's first step on the road to self-understanding can be seen as the recognition that he or she exists. This is an aspect of the self that he labelled 'self-as-subject', and he gave it various elements. These included an awareness of one's own agency (i.e. one's power to act), and an awareness of one's distinctiveness from other people. These features gradually emerge as infants explore their world and interact with caregivers. Cooley (1902) suggested that a sense of the self-as-subject was primarily concerned with being able to exercise power. He proposed that the earliest examples of this are an infant's attempts to control physical objects, such as toys or his or her own limbs. This is followed by attempts to affect the behaviour of other people. For example, infants learn that when they cry or smile someone responds to them.

C   Another powerful source of information for infants about the effects they can have on the world around them is provided when others mimic them. Many parents spend a lot of time, particularly in the early months, copying their infant's vocalizations and expressions. In addition, young children enjoy looking in mirrors, where the movements they can see are dependent upon their own movements. This is not to say that infants recognize the reflection as their *own* image (a later development). However, Lewis and Brooks-Gunn (1979) suggest that infants' developing understanding that the movements they see in the mirror are contingent on their own, leads to a growing awareness that they are distinct from other people. This is because they, and only they, can change the reflection in the mirror.

D   This understanding that children gain of themselves as active agents continues to develop in their attempts to co-operate with others in play. Dunn (1988) points out that it is in such day-to-day relationships and interactions that the child's understanding of his- or herself emerges. Empirical investigations of the self-as-subject in young children are, however, rather scarce because of difficulties of communication: even if young infants can reflect on their experience, they certainly cannot express this aspect of the self directly.

E   Once children have acquired a certain level of self-awareness, they begin to place themselves in a whole series of categories, which together play such an important part in defining them uniquely as 'themselves'. This second step in the development of a full sense of self is what James called the 'self-as-object'. This has been seen by many to be the aspect of the self which is most influenced by social elements, since it is made up of social roles (such as student, brother, colleague) and characteristics which derive their meaning from comparison or interaction with other people (such as trustworthiness, shyness, sporting ability).

F   Cooley and other researchers suggested a close connection between a person's own understanding of their identity and other people's understanding of it. Cooley believed that people build up their sense of identity from the reactions of others to them, and from the view they believe others have of them. He called the self-as-object the 'looking-glass self', since people come to see themselves as they are reflected in others. Mead (1934) went even further, and saw the self and the social world as inextricably bound together: 'The self is essentially a social structure, and it arises in social experience … it is impossible to conceive of a self arising outside of social experience.'

G   Lewis and Brooks-Gunn argued that an important developmental milestone is reached when children become able to recognize themselves visually without the support of seeing contingent movement. This recognition occurs around their second birthday. In one experiment, Lewis and Brooks-Gunn (1979) dabbed some red powder on the noses of children who were playing in front of a mirror, and then observed how often they touched their noses. The psychologists reasoned that if the children knew what they usually looked like, they would be surprised by the unusual red mark and would start touching it. On the other hand, they found that children of 15 to 18 months are generally not able to recognize themselves unless other cues such as movement are present.

H   Finally, perhaps the most graphic expressions of self-awareness in general can be seen in the displays of rage which are most common from 18 months to 3 years of age. In a longitudinal study of groups of three or four children, Bronson (1975) found that the intensity of the frustration and anger in their disagreements increased sharply between the ages of 1 and 2 years. Often, the children's disagreements involved a struggle over a toy that none of them had played with before or after the tug-of-war: the children seemed to be disputing ownership rather than wanting to play with it. Although it may be less marked in other societies, the link between the sense of 'self' and of 'ownership' is a notable feature of childhood in Western societies.

Questions 14–19

Reading Passage 2 has eight paragraphs, **A–H**.

Which paragraph contains the following information?

*Write the correct letter, **A–H**, in boxes 14–19 on your answer sheet.*

NB *You may use any letter more than once.*

14 an account of the method used by researchers in a particular study

15 the role of imitation in developing a sense of identity

16 the age at which children can usually identify a static image of themselves

17 a reason for the limitations of scientific research into 'self-as-subject'

18 reference to a possible link between culture and a particular form of behaviour

19 examples of the wide range of features that contribute to the sense of 'self-as-object'

Test 4

Questions 20–23

Look at the following findings (Questions 20–23) and the list of researchers below.

Match each finding with the correct researcher or researchers, A–E.

Write the correct letter, A–E, in boxes 20–23 on your answer sheet.

20   A sense of identity can never be formed without relationships with other people.

21   A child's awareness of self is related to a sense of mastery over things and people.

22   At a certain age, children's sense of identity leads to aggressive behaviour.

23   Observing their own reflection contributes to children's self awareness.

List of Researchers

A   James
B   Cooley
C   Lewis and Brooks-Gunn
D   Mead
E   Bronson

Test 4

Questions 20–23

Look at the following findings (Questions 20–23) and the list of researchers below.

Match each finding with the correct researcher or researchers, A–E.

Write the correct letter, A–E, in boxes 20–23 on your answer sheet.

20   A sense of identity can never be formed without relationships with other people.

21   A child's awareness of self is related to a sense of mastery over things and people.

22   At a certain age, children's sense of identity leads to aggressive behaviour.

23   Observing their own reflection contributes to children's self awareness.

List of Researchers

A   James
B   Cooley
C   Lewis and Brooks-Gunn
D   Mead
E   Bronson

Questions 24–26

Complete the summary below.

*Choose **ONE WORD ONLY** from the passage for each answer.*

Write your answers in boxes 24–26 on your answer sheet.

How children acquire a sense of identity

First, children come to realise that they can have an effect on the world around them, for example by handling objects, or causing the image to move when they face a **24** .... This aspect of self-awareness is difficult to research directly, because of **25** .... problems.

Secondly, children start to become aware of how they are viewed by others. One important stage in this process is the visual recognition of themselves which usually occurs when they reach the age of two. In Western societies at least, the development of self awareness is often linked to a sense of **26** .... , and can lead to disputes.

READING PASSAGE 3

*You should spend about 20 minutes on **Questions 27–40**, which are based on Reading Passage 3 on the following pages.*

Questions 27–30

Reading Passage 3 has six paragraphs, **A–F**.

*Choose the correct heading for paragraphs **B–E** from the list of headings below.*

*Write the correct number, **i–vii**, in boxes 27–30 on your answer sheet.*

List of Headings

i	Commercial pressures on people in charge
ii	Mixed views on current changes to museums
iii	Interpreting the facts to meet visitor expectations
iv	The international dimension
v	Collections of factual evidence
vi	Fewer differences between public attractions
vii	Current reviews and suggestions

Example	*Answer*
Paragraph **A**	**v**

27   Paragraph **B**

28   Paragraph **C**

29   Paragraph **D**

30   Paragraph **E**

The Development of Museums

A The conviction that historical relics provide infallible testimony about the past is rooted in the nineteenth and early twentieth centuries, when science was regarded as objective and value free. As one writer observes: 'Although it is now evident that artefacts are as easily altered as chronicles, public faith in their veracity endures: a tangible relic seems *ipso facto* real.' Such conviction was, until recently, reflected in museum displays. Museums used to look – and some still do – much like storage rooms of objects packed together in showcases: good for scholars who wanted to study the subtle differences in design, but not for the ordinary visitor, to whom it all looked alike. Similarly, the information accompanying the objects often made little sense to the lay visitor. The content and format of explanations dated back to a time when the museum was the exclusive domain of the scientific researcher.

B Recently, however, attitudes towards history and the way it should be presented have altered. The key word in heritage display is now 'experience', the more exciting the better and, if possible, involving all the senses. Good examples of this approach in the UK are the Jorvik Centre in York; the National Museum of Photography, Film and Television in Bradford; and the Imperial War Museum in London. In the US the trend emerged much earlier: Williamsburg has been a prototype for many heritage developments in other parts of the world. No one can predict where the process will end. On so-called heritage sites the re-enactment of historical events is increasingly popular, and computers will soon provide virtual reality experiences, which will present visitors with a vivid image of the period of their choice, in which they themselves can act as if part of the historical environment. Such developments have been criticised as an intolerable vulgarisation, but the success of many historical theme parks and similar locations suggests that the majority of the public does not share this opinion.

C In a related development, the sharp distinction between museum and heritage sites on the one hand, and theme parks on the other, is gradually evaporating. They already borrow ideas and concepts from one another. For example, museums have adopted story lines for exhibitions, sites have accepted 'theming' as a relevant tool, and theme parks are moving towards more authenticity and research-based presentations. In zoos, animals are no longer kept in cages, but in great spaces, either in the open air or in enormous greenhouses, such as the jungle and desert environments in Burgers' Zoo in Holland. This particular trend is regarded as one of the major developments in the presentation of natural history in the twentieth century.

D   Theme parks are undergoing other changes, too, as they try to present more serious social and cultural issues, and move away from fantasy. This development is a response to market forces and, although museums and heritage sites have a special, rather distinct, role to fulfil, they are also operating in a very competitive environment, where visitors make choices on how and where to spend their free time. Heritage and museum experts do not have to invent stories and recreate historical environments to attract their visitors: their assets are already in place. However, exhibits must be both based on artefacts and facts as we know them, and attractively presented. Those who are professionally engaged in the art of interpreting history are thus in a difficult position, as they must steer a narrow course between the demands of 'evidence' and 'attractiveness', especially given the increasing need in the heritage industry for income-generating activities.

E   It could be claimed that in order to make everything in heritage more 'real', historical accuracy must be increasingly altered. For example, *Pithecanthropus erectus* is depicted in an Indonesian museum with Malay facial features, because this corresponds to public perceptions. Similarly, in the Museum of Natural History in Washington, Neanderthal man is shown making a dominant gesture to his wife. Such presentations tell us more about contemporary perceptions of the world than about our ancestors. There is one compensation, however, for the professionals who make these interpretations: if they did not provide the interpretation, visitors would do it for themselves, based on their own ideas, misconceptions and prejudices. And no matter how exciting the result, it would contain a lot more bias than the presentations provided by experts.

F   Human bias is inevitable, but another source of bias in the representation of history has to do with the transitory nature of the materials themselves. The simple fact is that not everything from history survives the historical process. Castles, palaces and cathedrals have a longer lifespan than the dwellings of ordinary people. The same applies to the furnishings and other contents of the premises. In a town like Leyden in Holland, which in the seventeenth century was occupied by approximately the same number of inhabitants as today, people lived within the walled town, an area more than five times smaller than modern Leyden. In most of the houses several families lived together in circumstances beyond our imagination. Yet in museums, fine period rooms give only an image of the lifestyle of the upper class of that era. No wonder that people who stroll around exhibitions are filled with nostalgia; the evidence in museums indicates that life was so much better in the past. This notion is induced by the bias in its representation in museums and heritage centres.

Questions 31–36

Choose the correct letter, A, B, C or D.

Write the correct letter in boxes 31–36 on your answer sheet.

31 Compared with today's museums, those of the past

    A   did not present history in a detailed way.
    B   were not primarily intended for the public.
    C   were more clearly organised.
    D   preserved items with greater care.

32 According to the writer, current trends in the heritage industry

    A   emphasise personal involvement.
    B   have their origins in York and London.
    C   rely on computer images.
    D   reflect minority tastes.

33 The writer says that museums, heritage sites and theme parks

    A   often work in close partnership.
    B   try to preserve separate identities.
    C   have similar exhibits.
    D   are less easy to distinguish than before.

34 The writer says that in preparing exhibits for museums, experts

    A   should pursue a single objective.
    B   have to do a certain amount of language translation.
    C   should be free from commercial constraints.
    D   have to balance conflicting priorities.

35 In paragraph E, the writer suggests that some museum exhibits

    A   fail to match visitor expectations.
    B   are based on the false assumptions of professionals.
    C   reveal more about present beliefs than about the past.
    D   allow visitors to make more use of their imagination.

36 The passage ends by noting that our view of history is biased because

    A   we fail to use our imagination.
    B   only very durable objects remain from the past.
    C   we tend to ignore things that displease us.
    D   museum exhibits focus too much on the local area.

Questions 37–40

Do the following statements agree with the information given in Reading Passage 3?

In boxes 37–40 on your answer sheet, write

TRUE	*if the statement agrees with the information*
FALSE	*if the statement contradicts the information*
NOT GIVEN	*if there is no information on this*

37 Consumers prefer theme parks which avoid serious issues.

38 More people visit museums than theme parks.

39 The boundaries of Leyden have changed little since the seventeenth century.

40 Museums can give a false impression of how life used to be.

WRITING

WRITING TASK 1

You should spend about 20 minutes on this task.

The graph below gives information from a 2008 report about consumption of energy in the USA since 1980 with projections until 2030.

Summarise the information by selecting and reporting the main features, and make comparisons where relevant.

Write at least 150 words.

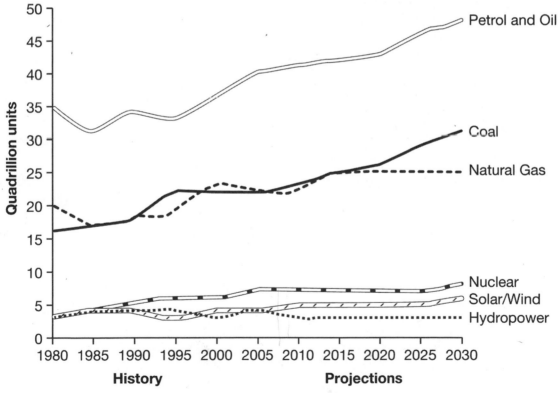

U.S. Energy Consumption by Fuel (1980–2030)

WRITING TASK 2

You should spend about 40 minutes on this task.

Write about the following topic:

Every year several languages die out. Some people think that this is not important because life will be easier if there are fewer languages in the world.

To what extent do you agree or disagree with this opinion?

Give reasons for your answer and include any relevant examples from your own knowledge or experience.

Write at least 250 words.

SPEAKING

PART 1

The examiner asks the candidate about him/herself, his/her home, work or studies and other familiar topics.

EXAMPLE

Bicycles

- How popular are bicycles in your home town? [Why?]
- How often do you ride a bicycle? [Why/Why not?]
- Do you think that bicycles are suitable for all ages? [Why/Why not?]
- What are the advantages of a bicycle compared to a car? [Why?]

PART 2

Describe a person who has done a lot of work to help people.

You should say:
who this person is/was
where this person lives/lived
what he/she has done to help people
and explain how you know about this person.

You will have to talk about the topic for one to two minutes.
You have one minute to think about what you are going to say.
You can make some notes to help you if you wish.

PART 3

Discussion topics:

Helping other people in the community

Example questions:
What are some of the ways people can help others in the community? Which is most important?
Why do you think some people like to help other people?
Some people say that people help others in the community more now than they did in the past. Do you agree or disagree? Why?

Community Services

Example questions:
What types of services, such as libraries or health centres, are available to the people who live in your area? Do you think there are enough of them?
Which groups of people generally need most support in a community? Why?
Who do you think should pay for the services that are available to the people in a community? Should it be the government or individual people?

General Training Reading and Writing Test A

READING

SECTION 1   *Questions 1–14*

Read the text below and answer Questions 1–6.

A

HELP – snack bar serving person

Bright, friendly, experience not essential
Energy and enthusiasm an absolute must
Sat & Sun only
Call or drop in at Kingsway Centre, Melbourn/Royston.
Tel: 01763 24272 and ask for the Manager.

B

Granta Hotel

requires a part-time silver service waiter/waitress.

Only applicants with experience
and good references need apply.
Excellent wages, meals on duty.
Tel: 01223 51468 (office hours)

C

WANTED from January till July, a nanny/carer for Toby, 2 yrs. Formal qualifications not as important as a sensible, warm and imaginative approach.

Hours: 8.30-5.00 Mon-Fri
Car driver essential, non smoker
References required
For further details phone: 01480 88056 after 6pm.

D

Cleaner required for 12-floor modern office block in the Station Road area, St Ives.

2 hours per day. Mondays to Fridays –
to finish work before the offices open

Wages: £80 per week
Tel: 01223 93292

E

Mature, experienced Administrator/Secretary

for soft furnishing company, working
within the hotel industry

Hours: 1pm – 5pm, Mon – Fri

Phone: Mr S Quinn 01353 71251

F

FULL-TIME COOK for a new and exciting café venture.
Good conditions. Pay and hours can be negotiated.

Apply Red Cafe (01863) 72052

G

50-Seater Restaurant
TO LET

Ideal for very experienced person looking to
start up on their own.

Located on busy A10 road.
Reply Box No. P762, Newmarket Newspapers Ltd.,
51 Cambridge Road, Newmarket, CB8 3BN

Questions 1–6

*Look at the seven job advertisements, **A–G**, on page 104 and read the descriptions of people below.*

Which is the most suitable job for each person?

*Write the correct letter, **A–G**, in boxes 1–6 on your answer sheet.*

1   a person with two small children who wants a few hours a week of unskilled work in the early mornings

2   a person with no experience or qualifications who is looking for a short term full-time job, Monday to Friday

3   a lively student with no experience, who cannot work on weekdays

4   a person with more than 20 years' experience in catering who would like to run a business

5   a catering college graduate who is now looking for his first full-time job

6   a person with many years' experience working in hotels who is now looking for well-paid part-time employment in a hotel

Read the text below and answer Questions 7–14.

INTERCITY Sleeper between London and Scotland

Most tickets may be used for travel by *Sleeper*, subject to availability, and a reservation in a two-berth cabin can be made for £25, except in the case of Solo and Special tickets, which include *Sleeper* reservations in the fare. The price includes early morning tea or coffee and biscuits. A continental or hot breakfast can be ordered if you wish.

Choose from a range of tickets to suit your journey.

A – SuperApex
Only available for travel after 9am. Book at least 2 weeks ahead and travel between Edinburgh or Glasgow and London for the unbeatable price of £59 return. This ticket is non-refundable 'unless the service is cancelled.

B – Apex
A real bargain fare. Only £69 return between Edinburgh or Glasgow and London. Great value *Sleeper* travel available by booking at least a week before outward travel. Ticket refundable on payment of a 25% administrative charge.

C – SuperSaver
Available right up to the day of travel and valid any day except these peak days: all Fridays, also 18-30 December, 31 March and 28 May. Departures between midnight and 2am count as previous day's departures. London to Glasgow or Edinburgh £82.

D – Saver
This flexible ticket is valid every day and can be bought on the day of travel. Your ticket allows standard class travel on any train between 10am and midnight. No seat reservations available. London to Glasgow or Edinburgh £95.

E – Solo
Treat yourself and enjoy exclusive use of a Standard cabin. Solo is an inclusive return travel ticket with *Sleeper* reservations for one or both directions. Outward and return reservations should be made at the time of booking. The journey must include a Saturday night away. £140-£160 London to Edinburgh/Glasgow return.

F – Special
Special is an inclusive return travel package for two people including sleeper reservations for one or both directions. It can mean savings for both of you. Outward and return reservations should be made at the time of booking. From £120.

G – Standard
Not the cheapest option but available up to the time of travel and valid for all trains and at all times. You are advised to turn up early for travel on a Friday.

Questions 7–14

*Look at the seven types of train ticket, **A–G**, on page 107.*

For which type of train ticket are the following statements true?

*Write the correct letter, **A–G**, in boxes 7–14 on your answer sheet.*

NB *You may use any letter more than once.*

7   There are advantages if you book a journey with a friend.

8   You cannot use this on a Friday.

9   This can be used without restriction.

10 This can only be booked up to 7 days before departure.

11 It's the cheapest ticket available but there is a restriction on departure time.

12 If you decide not to travel after you have bought the ticket, you cannot get your money back.

13 This is not available if you're travelling out on a Monday and back the next day.

14 You cannot use this ticket for departures between midnight and 10am.

SECTION 2   *Questions 15–27*

Read the text below and answer Questions 15–21.

FORMAL DRESS CODE FOR COMPANY EMPLOYEES

At TransitEuropean, the company's objective in establishing a formal dress code is to enable our employees to project the professional image that is in keeping with the needs of our clients and customers who seek our guidance, input, and professional services. Because our industry requires the appearance of trusted business professionals and we serve clients at our site on a daily basis, a more formal dress code is necessary for our employees.

Formal Dress Code Guidelines

In a formal business environment, the standard of dressing for men and women is a suit. Alternatively a jacket may be worn with appropriate accessories. Torn, dirty, or frayed clothing is unacceptable. Clothing should be pressed and never wrinkled. No dress code can cover all contingencies so employees must exert a certain amount of judgement in their choice of clothing to wear to work. If you experience uncertainty, please ask your supervisor for advice.

Shoes and Footwear

Conservative walking shoes, dress shoes, loafers, boots, flats, dress heels, and backless shoes are acceptable for work. Not wearing stockings or socks is inappropriate. Tennis shoes and any shoe with an open toe are not acceptable in the office.

Accessories and Jewellery

The wearing of ties, scarves, belts, and jewellery is encouraged, provided they are tasteful. Items which are flashy should be avoided.

Makeup, Perfume, and Cologne

A professional appearance is encouraged and excessive makeup is unprofessional. Remember that some employees may have allergic reactions to the chemicals in perfumes and makeup, so wear these substances in moderation.

Hats and Head Covering

Hats are not appropriate in the office. Head covers that are required for reasons of faith or to honour cultural tradition are permitted.

Dress Down Days

Certain days can be declared dress down days, generally Fridays. On these days, business casual clothing is allowed. Clothing that has our company logo is strongly encouraged. Sports team, university, and fashion brand names on clothing are generally acceptable. However, you may wish to keep a jacket in your office in case a client unexpectedly appears.

Violation of Dress Code

If clothing fails to meet these standards, as determined by the employee's supervisor, the employee will be asked not to wear the inappropriate item to work again. If the problem persists, the employee will receive a verbal warning and may be sent home to change clothes.

Questions 15–21

Complete the notes below.

*Choose **NO MORE THAN TWO WORDS** from the text for each answer.*

Write your answers in boxes 15–21 on your answer sheet.

NOTES ON COMPANY DRESS CODE

Aim of formal dress code: to present a **15** .... to clients

Acceptable types of formal clothing: jacket or suit

State of clothes: they must be **16** .... and in good condition

Footwear: tennis shoes and open toe shoes are not allowed

Accessories: ties, scarves, belts and jewellery may be worn

– these must be **17** .... and not brightly coloured

Make up: avoid wearing too much make up and perfume

– these sometimes cause **18** ....

Hats: hats should not be worn

– head covers in line with religious reasons or **19** .... are allowed

Dressing down: casual clothing is allowed on some Fridays

– clothing with the **20** .... on it is recommended

Breaking the dress code: if advice is repeatedly ignored, a **21** .... is given

Read the text below and answer Questions 22–27.

JLP RETAIL: STAFF BENEFITS

Whatever your role, your pay range will be extremely competitive and reviewed in the light of your progress. In addition to your salary, you will enjoy an array of excellent benefits from the moment you join the company.

Paid holiday
The holiday entitlement is four weeks per year, rising to five weeks after three years (or in the case of IT graduate trainees, after promotion to programmer or trainee analyst). There are further long-service increases for most staff after ten or fifteen years. Managers, including graduate trainees, receive five weeks' holiday from the outset.

Pension scheme
We offer a non-contributory final salary pension scheme, payable from the age of 60, to most staff who have completed the qualifying period of five years.

Life assurance
Our life assurance scheme pays a sum equivalent to three times your annual salary to your nominated beneficiary.

Discounts
After three months' service, all staff are entitled to a 12% discount on most purchases from the company's stores. This rises to 25% after one year's service.

Subsidised dining room
In most sites, we provide a dining room where you can enjoy excellent food at very reasonable prices.

Holiday and leisure facilities
The business owns a number of residential clubs which offer subsidised holiday accommodation for staff with at least three years' service.

Sports clubs
We support an extensive range of sports activities including football, netball, golf, skiing, sailing, squash, riding and gliding.

Ticket subsidies
Ticket subsidies of 50% of the cost of plays or concerts are available. Staff may also take advantage of corporate membership to bodies such as the Science Museum.

Education subsidies
We give generous financial support to staff who wish to acquire leisure skills or continue their education, e.g. through the Open University or evening classes.

Extended leave
Staff who complete 25 years' service can enjoy paid sabbatical leave of up to six months.

Health services
We have an occupational health service staffed by full-time doctors and health advisers.

Financial help, benefits and discounted deals
In cases of particular hardship, we will help staff with a loan. We have also negotiated a range of benefits for staff such as discounted private healthcare and a car purchase scheme, along with a number of one-off deals with hotels and amusement parks.

Questions 22–27

Complete the sentences below.

Choose **NO MORE THAN TWO WORDS AND/OR A NUMBER** *from the text for each answer.*

Write your answers in boxes 22–27 on your answer sheet.

22   Pay increases depend on the .... that each member of staff makes.

23   Employees must work a minimum of .... to be eligible for a pension.

24   Staff may take a holiday at one of the .... provided by the company.

25   The company pay half the seat price for .... and plays.

26   The company gives financial assistance for both educational courses and .... as part of staff development.

27   Employees may be entitled to a .... if they find themselves in difficult circumstances.

SECTION 3   *Questions 28–40*

Read the text on pages 113 and 114 and answer questions 28–40.

OUT OF THE ASHES

A   On the afternoon of 30th August 1989, fire broke out at Uppark, a large eighteenth-century house in Sussex. For a year builders had been replacing the lead on the roof, and by a stroke of irony, were due to finish the next day, on August 31st. Within fifteen minutes of the alarm being sounded, the fire brigade had arrived on the scene, though nothing was to survive of the priceless collection on the first floor apart from an oil painting of a dog which the firemen swept up as they finally retreated from the blaze. But due to the courage and swift action of the previous owners, the Meade-Featherstonhaugh family, and the staff, stewards and visitors to the house, who formed human chains to pass the precious pieces of porcelain, furniture and paintings out on to the lawn, 95 per cent of the contents from the ground floor and the basement were saved. As the fire continued to rage, the National Trust's conservators were being mobilised, and that evening local stationers were especially opened to provide the bulk supplies of blotting paper so desperately needed in the salvage operation.

B   The following morning, Uppark stood open to the sky. A sludge of wet charcoal covered the ground floor and basement, and in every room charred and fallen timbers lay amongst the smoke. It was a scene of utter devastation.

C   After the initial sense of shock, the days which followed the fire were filled with discoveries. Helped by volunteers, the National Trust's archaeologists and conservators swung into action, first of all marking the site out into a grid and then salvaging everything down to the last door handle. The position of each fragment was recorded, and all the debris was stored in countless dustbins before being sifted and categorised.

D   There was great excitement as remnants of the lantern from the Staircase Hall were pulled out from the debris of two fallen floors, and also three weeks later when the Red Room carpet, thought to have been totally lost, was found wrapped around the remains of a piano. There was a lucky reprieve for the State Bed too. Staff who had left the scene at 3am on the night of the fire had thought its loss was inevitable, but when they returned the next morning it had escaped largely undamaged. Firemen, directed by the National Trust's conservators from outside the Tapestry Room window, dismantled the silk-hung bed and passed it out piece by piece. Twenty minutes later the ceiling fell in.

E   The scale of the task to repair Uppark was unprecedented in the National Trust. The immediate question was whether it should be done at all. A decision had to be taken quickly, as the building was unsound and whatever had not been damaged by the fire was exposed to the elements. Within a month, after consulting many experts and with the agreement of the National Trust's Executive Committee, the restoration programme began. It was undertaken for three main reasons. After the fire it had become apparent just how much remained of the structure with its splendidly decorated interiors; to have pulled the house down, as one commentator suggested, would have been vandalism. Also the property was covered by insurance, so the repairs would not call upon the National Trust's own funds. Lastly, much had been saved of the fine collection acquired especially for Uppark from 1747 by Sir Matthew Featherstonhaugh and his son Harry. These objects belonged nowhere else, and complete restoration of the house would allow them to be seen and enjoyed again in their original setting.

F   The search for craftsmen and women capable of doing the intricate restoration work was nation-wide. Once the quality and skill of the individual or company had been ascertained, they had to pass an economic test, as every job was competitively tendered. This has had enormous benefits because not only have a number of highly skilled people come to the fore – woodcarvers for example, following in the footsteps of Grinling Gibbons – but many of them, for example plasterers, have relearnt the skills of the seventeenth and eighteenth centuries which can now be of use to other country house owners when the need arises.

G   In June 1994 the building programme was completed, on time and on budget. The total cost of the work to repair the house and its contents came to be nearly £20 million, largely met from insurance. In addition, it made economic sense for the National Trust to invest time and money in upgrading water and heating systems, installing modern environmental controls, and updating fire and security equipment.

H   The final stages of restoration and the massive programme of reinstallation took eight months. The family and the room stewards were visibly moved when returning to their old haunts, perhaps the best testament that the spirit of Uppark had not died. But the debate will no doubt continue as to whether or not it was right to repair the house after the fire. The National Trust has done its best to remain true to Uppark; it is for others to judge the success of the project.

Note: The National Trust is a charitable organisation in Britain set up over a hundred years ago to preserve the national heritage.

Questions 28–33

The text on pages 113 and 114 has eight paragraphs, **A–H**.

Which paragraphs contain the following information?

*Write the appropriate letters, **A–H**, in boxes 28–33 on your answer sheet.*

28   the procedure for sorting through the remains of the fire

29   how Uppark looked after the fire

30   improvements made to the rebuilt Uppark

31   the selection of people to carry out the repair work

32   why the National Trust chose to rebuild Uppark

33   how people reacted to the rebuilt Uppark

Questions 34–37

Answer the questions below.

*Choose **NO MORE THAN THREE WORDS** from the text for each answer.*

Write your answers in boxes 34–37 on your answer sheet.

34   On what date in 1989 should the original repairs to the roof have been completed?

35   By what method were things rescued immediately from the burning house?

36   After the fire, what did the conservators require large quantities of immediately?

37   Into what did the conservators put material recovered from the fire?

Questions 38–40

*Choose the correct letter, **A**, **B**, **C** or **D**.*

Write the correct letter in boxes 38–40 on your answer sheet.

38   The fire destroyed

    A   all the contents of the ground floor.
    B   most of the contents of the basement.
    C   the roof of the house.
    D   all the contents of the first floor.

39   One of the reasons the National Trust decided to rebuild Uppark was that

    A   the Meade-Featherstonhaugh family wanted them to.
    B   the building as it stood was unsound.
    C   they wouldn't have to pay for the repairs.
    D   nothing on this scale had been tried before.

40   Some of the craftsmen and women employed in the restoration of Uppark have benefited because

    A   they were very well paid for doing intricate work.
    B   their businesses have become more competitive.
    C   they were able to work with Grinling Gibbons.
    D   they acquired skills they didn't have previously.

WRITING

WRITING TASK 1

You should spend about 20 minutes on this task.

> *You are working for a company. You need to take some time off work and want to ask your manager about this.*
>
> *Write a letter to your manager. In your letter*
> * *explain why you want to take time off work*
> * *give details of the amount of time you need*
> * *suggest how your work could be covered while you are away*

Write at least 150 words.

You do **NOT** need to write any addresses.

Begin your letter as follows:

Dear .... ,

WRITING TASK 2

You should spend about 40 minutes on this task.

Write about the following topic:

> *Being a celebrity – such as a famous film star or sports personality – brings problems as well as benefits.*
>
> *Do you think that being a celebrity brings more benefits or more problems?*

Give reasons for your answer and include any relevant examples from your own knowledge or experience.

Write at least 250 words.

General Training Reading and Writing Test B

SECTION 1   Questions 1–14

Read the text below and answer Questions 1–7.

The Young Person's Railcard

A Young Person's Railcard gives young people the opportunity to purchase discounted rail tickets across Britain. Just imagine where it could take you – to festivals, to see distant friends or to London for a weekend break.

Who can apply?

Absolutely anybody between 16 and 25 can apply. You will need to provide proof that you are under 26 years of age. For this, only your birth certificate, driving licence, passport or medical card will be acceptable. Alternatively, if you are a mature student over this age but in full-time education, you can also apply. In order to prove your eligibility, you will need to get your headteacher, tutor, or head of department to sign the application form as well as one of your photos, the latter also needing to be officially stamped. 'Full-time education' is defined as over 15 hours per week for at least 20 weeks a year.

Then go along to any major railway station, rail-appointed travel agent or authorised student travel office with your completed application form from this leaflet, together with £28, two passport-sized photos and proof of eligibility.

Using your railcard

You can use it at any time – weekends, Bank Holidays or during the week. But if you travel before 10 am Monday to Friday (except during July and August) minimum fares will apply. For full details of these, please ask at your local station or contact a rail-appointed travel agent.

Conditions

In cases where a railcard does not bear the user's signature, it will be treated as invalid. Neither your railcard nor any tickets bought with it may be used by anybody else. Unless there are no purchase facilities available at the station where you began your journey, you will be required to pay the full fare if you are unable to produce a valid ticket for inspection during a journey.

Reduced rate tickets are not available for first-class travel or for Eurostar links to France and Belgium. Passengers will be charged the full rate if they want to use these services.

Questions 1–7

Complete the sentences below.

*Choose **NO MORE THAN THREE WORDS** from the text for each answer.*

Write your answers in boxes 1–7 on your answer sheet.

1   Railcard applicants over 25 need to be involved in ....

2   For mature, full-time students, one of the photographs submitted must be signed and ....

3   At certain times of the year, there are no .... for railcard holders at any time of day.

4   If your railcard doesn't have your .... it will be impossible to use it for travel.

5   The benefits of a railcard are not transferable to ....

6   If you have no ticket but boarded a train at a station without any .... you will still be eligible for a discounted ticket.

7   If railcard holders wish to use the Eurostar network they must pay the ....

Read the text below and answer Questions 8–14.

TRAIN TRAVEL INFORMATION

We offer several distinct options for you to choose the ticket that suits you best.

TICKET TYPE	DISCOUNT*	NOTES
standard returns	20%	return within 60 days of outward trip
same day returns	25%	ticket cannot be altered or refunded
children	40%	children between 4 and 11
students	25%	student card must be shown
senior citizens	25%	seniors card must be shown
groups (10–25 people)	15%	discount on each section of the trip
globe-trotter tickets	according to ticket	Railpass, Tourist Card, Econopass

* Only one discount may apply to each fare.

CHANGES AND REFUNDS

Tickets may be refunded not later than 5 minutes before the departure of the train for a charge of 15% of the ticket price, or the journey may be changed to another day for a charge of 10% of the ticket price. (Not applicable to same day returns.)

CHANGES FOR SAME DAY TRAVEL

You may change your ticket once without charge for a journey on the same day as the original ticket.

INFORMATION OF INTEREST TO TRAVELLERS

- When you buy your ticket it is up to you to check that the dates and times of the journey on it are exactly as you requested.
- Ticket control and access to each train platform will be open until 2 minutes before departure of the train.
- Each traveller may take one suitcase and one item of hand luggage. You may also check in 15kgs. of luggage not later than 30 minutes before departure, at no extra charge.
- If you would like to charter a train, or make reservations for over 25 passengers travelling together, call the Sales Department.

OUR TIMETABLE IS GUARANTEED

If the arrival of your train at your destination is delayed by more than 5 minutes according to the timetable, we will refund the full price of your ticket if the delay is caused by our company

Questions 8–14

Complete the summary below.

*Choose **NO MORE THAN THREE WORDS** from the text for each answer.*

Write your answers in boxes 8–14 on your answer sheet.

An elderly person who is also studying full-time receives a concession of **8** ....

Large groups people who want to reserve seats should get in touch with the **9** ....

If travellers cancel their trip, they will usually receive back the ticket price less **10** .... , or they may change the date of their trip by paying **11** .... of the original value. These concessions do not apply in the case of **12** .... It is the passenger's responsibility to make sure the **13** .... and .... are correct.

Travellers should ensure they are ready to board the train with at least **14** .... to spare. They may take a suitcase with them in the carriage as well as hand luggage. A traveller may check in 15 kilos maximum weight of luggage but this must be done at least 30 minutes before the train leaves.

SECTION 2   *Questions 15–27*

Read the text below and answer Questions 15–20.

Professional Credentials:
Advice for Immigrants

As an immigrant to North America, you will need to ensure that employers and organisations such as colleges and universities properly recognise your international credentials. These may be trade certificates, but also educational qualifications such as degrees or diplomas, that you have completed or partially-completed.

It is common for hiring personnel to have little or no training in evaluating an academic background earned outside of North America. But at the same time, employers see formal education as very important when hiring. Education is a hiring requirement for 60% of employment opportunities, but 40% of human resources staff say that if they do not know a lot about the value of documents attained elsewhere, they will not recognise them.

Research has shown that sometimes immigrants start with a lower salary level than people who have completed their training in North America. You may want to apply for employment opportunities with companies whose staff understands your situation or, more importantly, who know where to send you to get your North American qualifications. If you need to complete your training in North America, apprenticeships leading to skilled trades are in high demand. Apprenticeship training is a hands-on program where about 10% is in a classroom setting at community colleges, and 90% of the training is on-the-job. The training involves working for an employer and earning income during the training period. Sometimes there is a limit of 5 years for training. You may be able to use this training toward college or university credits or education. There is a good potential for long-term job security after completion of apprenticeship training.

If you earned your papers outside of North America, you will need to get them translated if you want to work or study. It is important for you that your education is assessed by an accredited assessment service when you are applying for jobs, and particularly if the job posting has an education requirement. As well, it is recommended that you include a copy of the report with your cover letter. It is suggested that you provide this information early and do not wait until the time you actually meet with the employer. Getting job interviews is more than 50% of the whole process of securing employment; and with an evaluation report, you want to make sure that employers are screening you 'in' rather than 'out'.

Establishing yourself in North America is a difficult process, but companies do consider integrating immigrants into the workforce important to the workplace mosaic. Employers are making significant progress in improving diversity at work.

Questions 15–20

Complete the sentences below.

*Choose **NO MORE THAN TWO WORDS** from the text for each answer.*

Write your answers in boxes 15–20 on your answer sheet.

15 New arrivals to North America need to make sure that their academic qualifications or their .... are accepted.

16 A significant number of companies view .... as a major requirement.

17 People educated in North America may initially be offered a higher .... than immigrants.

18 .... courses often provide more job stability.

19 Most of the effort to find work is spent trying to obtain ....

20 As more newcomers enter the workforce, ... increases.

Read the text below and answer Questions 21–27.

How to Prepare for a Presentation

The first time your boss suggests that you formally present something to your department or a client, your reaction may be to panic. But remember that being asked to present is a compliment. Someone believes that you have valuable information to share with the group, and wants to listen to your ideas.

You need to decide exactly what you will say during the allotted time. Condense your topic into one sentence. What *do* you want your audience to remember or learn from your talk? This is your 'big idea'. Remember that you are dealing with the short attention spans of individuals who tend to have many things on their minds.

Think of three main points you want to make to support your overall topic. Develop a story to demonstrate each of those concepts. This could be something that happened to you or someone you know, or something you read in a newspaper or magazine.

We have all heard the saying *A picture is worth a thousand words*. Think about how your presentation can be more interesting to watch. Props are a wonderful way to make your talk come alive. You could do something as simple as holding up a toy phone receiver when talking about customer service or putting on a hat to signal a different part of your talk.

Think of a dynamic and unusual way to start your presentation. This might involve telling anecdotes that relate to your topic. Never begin with, 'Thank you for inviting me here to talk with you today.' You will put your audience to sleep right away. Start off enthusiastically so they will listen with curiosity and interest. After your energetic introduction, identify yourself briefly and thank the audience for taking the time to listen to you.

Plan your ending, and finish in a memorable way. Your listeners remember best what they hear at the beginning and end of a speech, so conclude with a game in which they can participate, or tell a humorous story and your audience will leave laughing.

Don't try to memorise your talk or read it word-for-word. It will sound stilted and boring. Instead, practise your dynamic introduction and conclusion until you can deliver them effortlessly. If you do this you'll feel a burst of confidence that will help you sail through the whole of the speech.

Questions 21–27

Complete the sentences below.

*Choose **ONE WORD ONLY** from the text for each answer.*

Write your answers in boxes 21–27 on your answer sheet.

How to Prepare for a Presentation

- You should regard an invitation to speak as a **21** ....

- Express your main idea in a **22** ....

- Try using a .... **23** to support the major points you are making.

- Add visual excitement to your talk by using **24** ....

- Express appreciation to your listeners for their **25** ....

- A **26** .... will get the audience to interact.

- It is important to prepare well as this will increase your **27** ....

SECTION 3   Questions 28–40

Read the text below and answer Questions 28–40.

The Birdmen

Will people finally be able to fly long distances without a plane?
John Andres *investigates*

People have dreamt of flying since written history began. In the 1400s, Leonardo da Vinci drew detailed plans for human flying machines. You might have thought the invention of mechanised flight would have put an end to such ideas. Far from it. For many enthusiasts, the ultimate flight fantasy is the jet pack, a small piece of equipment on your back which enables you to climb vertically into the air and fly forwards, backwards and turn. Eric Scott was a stuntman in Hollywood for about a decade and has strapped jet packs to his back more than 600 times and propelled himself hundreds of metres into the air. Now he works for an energy-drink company that pays him to travel around the world with his jet pack. As Scott says: 'I get to do what I love and wherever I go I advertise Go Fast drinks. Existing packs work for little more than 30 seconds, but people are working on designs which let you fly around for 20 minutes. That would be amazing,' says Scott.

Paramotoring is another way of getting into the air. It combines the sort of parachute used in paragliding with a small engine and propeller and is now becoming popular. Chris Clarke has been flying a paramotor for five years. 'Getting about is roughly comparable with driving a petrol-powered car in terms of expense. The trouble is that paramotoring is ill-suited to commuting because of the impossibility of taking off in strong winds,' says Clarke.

Another keen paramotorist recently experienced a close call when in the air. 'I started to get a warm feeling in my back,' says Patrick Vandenbulcke. 'I thought I was just sweating. But then I started to feel burning and I realized I had to get to the ground fast. After an inspection of the engine later, I noticed that the exhaust pipe had moved during the flight and the harness had started melting.' This hasn't put Vandenbulcke off, however, and he is enthusiastic about persuading others to take up paramotoring. However he warns: 'Although it seems cheaper to try to teach yourself, you will regret it later as you won't have a good technique.' A training course will cost over £1,000, while the equipment costs a few thousand pounds. You may pick up cheaper equipment secondhand, however. There was one pre-used kit advertised on a website, with a bit of damage to the cage and tips of the propellers due to a rough landing. 'Scared myself to death,' the seller reported, 'hence the reason for this sale.'

Fun though it is, paramotoring is not in the same league as the acrobatics demonstrated by Yves Rossy. He has always enjoyed being a daredevil showman. He once parachuted from a plane above Lake Geneva and, intentionally skimming the top of a fountain as he landed, he descended to the lake where he grabbed some water ski equipment and started waterskiing while the crowd watched open-mouthed.

Rossy, who has been labelled 'the Birdman', was born in 1959 in Switzerland. After flying planes for the air force from the ages of 20 to 28, he went on to do a job as a pilot with a commercial airline from 1988 to 2000. 'The cockpit of a plane is the most beautiful office in the world,' he says, 'but I didn't have any contact with the air around me. It was a bit like being in a box or a submarine under water.' From then on, he therefore concentrated on becoming the first jet-powered flying man.

In May 2008, he stepped out of an aircraft at about 3000 metres. Within seconds he was soaring and diving at over 290 kph, at one point reaching 300 kph, about 104 kph faster than the typical falling skydiver. His speed was monitored by a plane flying alongside. Rossy started his flight with a free fall, then he powered four jet turbines to keep him in the air before releasing a parachute which enabled him to float to the ground. The jet turbines are attached to special wings which he can unfold. The wings were manufactured by a German firm called JCT Composites. Initially he had approached a company called Jet-Kit which specialised in miniature planes, but the wings they made for him weren't rigid enough to support the weight of the engines. Rossy says he has become 'the first person to maintain a stable horizontal flight, thanks to aerodynamic carbon foldable wings.' Without these special wings, it is doubtful he would have managed to do this.

Rossy's ambitions include flying down the Grand Canyon. To do this, he will have to fit his wings with bigger, more powerful jets. The engines he currently uses already provide enough thrust to allow him to climb through the air, but then he needs the power to stay there. In terms of the physical strength involved, Rossy insists it's no more difficult than riding a motorbike. 'But even the slightest change in position can cause problems. I have to focus hard on relaxing in the air, because if you put tension in your body, you start to swing round.' If he makes it, other fliers will want to know whether they too will some day be able to soar. The answer is yes, possibly, but it is unlikely to be more than an expensive hobby.

Questions 28–30

*Choose the correct letter, **A**, **B**, **C** or **D**.*

Write the correct letter in boxes 28–30 on your answer sheet.

28 What information is given about Vandenbulcke in paragraph 3?

    A   He narrowly avoided a dangerous situation.
    B   He did not understand the equipment he was using.
    C   He did not react fast enough to the situation.
    D   He was fortunate to get the help he needed.

29 When the writer refers to some second-hand paramotoring equipment which was for sale, he is emphasising that

    A   paramotoring equipment is in short supply.
    B   paramotoring equipment needs to be carefully tested.
    C   paramotoring is a very expensive hobby.
    D   paramotoring can be a dangerous pastime.

30 The description of what happened at Lake Geneva is given to suggest that Rossy

    A   frequently changes his plans.
    B   likes to do what appears impossible.
    C   is an excellent overall sportsman.
    D   knows the area very thoroughly.

Questions 31–35

Complete the summary below.

*Choose **ONE WORD AND/OR A NUMBER** from the text for each answer.*

Write your answers in boxes 31–35 on your answer sheet.

Yves Rossy

Yves Rossy was born in 1959. He worked as both a military and **31** .... pilot before focusing on his ambition of becoming a jet-powered flying man. First he asked a firm which made **32** .... planes to construct some **33** .... for him, but these proved unsuitable. The second company he approached was able to help him, however. On a flight in May 2008, he managed to achieve a top speed of **34** .... easily exceeding the speed achieved by the average **35** .... He had engines to keep him in the air and then used a parachute when it was time to come down.

Questions 36–40

Look at the following statements (Questions 36–40) and the list of people below.

*Match each statement with the correct person, **A, B, C** or **D**.*

*Write the correct letter, **A, B, C** or **D**, in boxes 36–40 on your answer sheet.*

36   He acknowledges the role of his equipment in enabling him to set a flying record.

37   He explains how he uses his flying expertise to promote a product.

38   He explains what led him to experiment with different ways of flying.

39   He describes a mistake some beginners might make.

40   He mentions circumstances which prevent you from leaving the ground.

People
A   Eric Scott
B   Chris Clarke
C   Patrick Vandenbulcke
D   Yves Rossy

WRITING

WRITING TASK 1

You should spend about 20 minutes on this task.

> *On a recent holiday you lost a valuable item. Fortunately you have travel insurance to cover the cost of anything lost.*
>
> *Write a letter to the manager of your insurance company. In your letter*
> * *describe the item you lost*
> * *explain how you lost it*
> * *tell the insurance company what you would like them to do*

Write at least 150 words.

You do **NOT** need to write any addresses.

Begin your letter as follows:

Dear Sir or Madam,

WRITING TASK 2

You should spend about 40 minutes on this task.

Write about the following topic:

> *Some people think that the teenage years are the happiest times of most people's lives. Others think that adult life brings more happiness, in spite of greater responsibilities.*
>
> *Discuss both these views and give your own opinion.*

Give reasons for your answer and include any relevant examples from your own knowledge or experience.

Write at least 250 words.

Tapescripts

TEST 1

SECTION 1

WOMAN:	Good evening. King's <u>Restaurant</u>.	*Example*
MAN:	Good evening. I'm ringing about the job I understand you have vacant.	
WOMAN:	Oh yes.	
MAN:	I'd like to find out a few more details, if I may.	
WOMAN:	Yes, of course. Can I take your name?	
MAN:	It's Peter Chin.	
WOMAN:	Okay Peter. Well, if you want to ask about the job and then if we're both still interested, we could arrange for you to come for an interview.	
MAN:	Great, thanks. I'm afraid I missed the advert for the job but heard about it from a friend.	
WOMAN:	That's no problem at all. What would you like to know?	
MAN:	Well, um, what sort of work is it – washing up?	
WOMAN:	It's <u>answering the phone</u>.	Q1
MAN:	Oh right, fine.	
WOMAN:	And not waiting at table.	
MAN:	That'd be good. And how many nights a week would it be?	
WOMAN:	Well, we're really only busy at the weekend.	
MAN:	So two nights?	
WOMAN:	Three actually, so it would work out at twelve hours a week.	
MAN:	That'd be fine. It wouldn't interfere with my studies.	
WOMAN:	Are you at the university?	
MAN:	Yes. First year Physics student.	
WOMAN:	Oh, right.	
MAN:	Um, and because I'm not an EU national would I need a work permit?	
WOMAN:	Yes you would. Just get your tutor to sign it.	
MAN:	That wouldn't be a problem, if I were to get the job. Um, where exactly is the restaurant?	
WOMAN:	Well, we have two branches – the one we're recruiting for is in <u>Hillsdunne Road</u>.	Q2
MAN:	I don't know that. How do you spell it please?	
WOMAN:	It's H-I-double L-S-D-U-double N-E Road.	
MAN:	Got that. Thanks. Is it near a bus stop?	
WOMAN:	Yes. <u>The nearest one would probably be just beside the Library</u>.	Q3
MAN:	Oh yes, I know it. That'd be fine for me. And could I ask about the pay?	
WOMAN:	We're offering <u>£4.45 an hour</u>.	Q4
MAN:	That's very good. My last job was £3.95 an hour.	

WOMAN:	We feel it's pretty good and we also offer some good fringe benefits.
MAN:	Really?
WOMAN:	Well, we give you a free dinner, so you eat well.
MAN:	Right, better than hostel food!

131

WOMAN:	We certainly hope so! And <u>we also offer extra pay for working on national holidays.</u>	Q5
MAN:	Oh, that's a really good perk, isn't it?	
WOMAN:	Yes, we think so. And then because of the difficulties of getting public transport, <u>if you're working after 11 o'clock we drive you home.</u>	Q6
MAN:	Oh, that's good to know.	
WOMAN:	Well, we'd certainly be interested in inviting you for an interview, if you're still interested?	
MAN:	Oh yes, certainly. Could I just also ask what qualities you're looking for?	
WOMAN:	Well, for this particular job <u>we want a clear voice</u>, which you obviously do have!	Q7
MAN:	Thanks.	
WOMAN:	And <u>you must be able to think quickly</u>, you know.	Q8
MAN:	Well, I hope I'd ...	
WOMAN:	So, when could you come in for an interview? We're actually quite quiet tonight?	
MAN:	Sorry, I couldn't come tonight. Or tomorrow, I'm afraid. Thursday's okay – that'd be <u>22nd of October</u>.	Q9
WOMAN:	Fine, after 5 p.m.?	
MAN:	Yes, fine. Would 6 o'clock be okay?	
WOMAN:	Perfect. And could you bring along the names of two referees?	
MAN:	Yes, that's fine, no problem.	
WOMAN:	Good. I look forward to seeing you.	
MAN:	Oh, by the way, who should I ask for?	
WOMAN:	Oh yes, of course, sorry. My name is Samira <u>Manuja</u>.	Q10
MAN:	Can you spell that, please?	
WOMAN:	M-A-N-U-J-A.	
MAN:	Okay, I've got that. Thanks very much.	
WOMAN:	Look forward to seeing you ...	

SECTION 2

ANDREW:	Now we go to Jane who is going to tell us about what's happening in town this weekend.	
JANE:	Right, thanks Andrew, and now on to what's new, and do we really need yet another sports shop in Bradcaster? Well, most of you probably know Sports World – <u>the branch of a Danish sports goods company</u> that opened a few years ago – it's attracted a lot of custom, and so the company has now decided to open another branch in the area. It's going to be in the shopping centre to <u>the west of Bradcaster</u>, so that will be good news for all of you who've found the original shop in the north of the town hard to get to.	Q11 Q12
	I was invited to a special preview and I can promise you, this is the ultimate in sports retailing. The whole place has been given a new minimalist look with the company's signature colours of black and red. <u>The first three floors have a huge range of sports clothing</u> as well as equipment, and on the top floor there's a café and a book and DVD section. You'll find all the well-known names as well as some less well-known ones. If they haven't got exactly what you want in stock they <u>promise to get it for you in ten days</u>. Unlike the other store, where it	Q13 Q14

can take up to fourteen days. They cover all the major sports, including football, tennis and swimming, but <u>they particularly focus on running</u>,   *Q15* and they claim to have the widest range of equipment in the country. As well as that, a whole section of <u>the third floor is devoted to sports bags</u>,   *Q16* including the latest designs from the States – if you can't find what you want here, it doesn't exist!

The shop will be open from 9.00 am this Saturday and if you go along to the opening then you'll have the chance to meet the national 400 metres running champion Paul King, who's coming along to open the shop, and <u>he will be staying around until about midday</u> to chat to any fans who want   *Q17* to meet him and sign autographs.

Then there will be a whole range of special attractions all weekend. There will be free tickets for local sporting events for the first 50 customers, and also a special competition open to all. Just answer fifteen out of twenty sports questions correctly to win a signed copy of Paul King's DVD 'Spring Tips', while <u>the first person to get all the questions correct gets a year's</u>   *Q18* <u>free membership of the Bradcaster Gym</u>. All entrants will receive a special Sports calendar with details of all Bradcaster fixtures in the coming year.

One of the special opening offers is a fitness test – a complete review of your cardiac fitness and muscle tone, actually done in the shop by qualified staff. <u>This would normally cost £30.00 but is available at half</u>   *Q19 & 20* <u>price for this month only. There are only a limited number of places</u> <u>available for this, so to make a booking</u> phone 560341. In addition, if you open an account you get lots more special offers including the chance to try out equipment at special open evenings …

SECTION 3

TEACHER:	Before we start, Spiros and Hiroko, thanks for coming in today to talk about your recent study experiences and congratulations to you both in doing so well in your first semester exams! I'd like to discuss with you the value of the English for Academic Purposes course you did here last year before starting your university course. Spiros, if I could start with you, what parts of the programme have now proved to be particularly valuable to you?
SPIROS:	I think that having to do a seminar presentation really helped me. For example, a couple of weeks ago in our marketing subject, when it was my turn to give a presentation I felt quite confident. Of course, I was still nervous but because I had done one before, I knew what to expect. Also, I know I was well-prepared and I had practised my timing. In fact, I think that in relation to some of the other people in my group, I did quite a good job because <u>my overall style was quite professional</u>. What about you, Hiroko? *Q21*
HIROKO:	Mmm, that's interesting. In my group, I was really surprised by the way the students did their presentations – they just read their notes aloud! Can you believe that? <u>They didn't worry about their presentation style</u> *Q22* <u>or keeping eye contact with their audience</u> – and I remember that these things were really stressed to us in the course here.
TEACHER:	So, how did you approach your presentation, Hiroko?

HIROKO:	Well, to speak frankly, I read my notes too! At the time, it was a relief to do it this way, but actually when I had finished, <u>I didn't feel any real sense of satisfaction</u>. I didn't feel positive about the experience at all.	Q23
SPIROS:	That's a pity. You know, although I was pleased with my presentation, <u>I am not so pleased with my actual performance right now in the tutorials</u> – during the whole semester I've not said anything in our tutorial discussions. Not a word.	Q24
HIROKO:	Really, Spiros? Why's that? Do the other students talk too much?	
SPIROS:	It's partly that, but it's mostly because I have had no confidence to speak out. Their style of speaking is so different – it's not the style we were used to during the course. They use so many colloquialisms, they're not very polite and sometimes there seems to be no order in their discussion. Also, <u>they are very familiar with each other, so because they know each other's habits, they can let each other into the discussion</u>.	Q25
HIROKO:	You're right, Spiros, I've experienced that too.	

HIROKO:	For most of this semester, I've said absolutely nothing in tutorials. But recently, <u>I've been trying to speak up more and I just jump in</u>, and I've noticed an interesting thing, I've noticed that if they thought my point was interesting or new, then the next time they actually asked for my opinion, and then it was much easier for me to be part of the discussion.	Q26
SPIROS:	That's great, Hiroko! I hope that happens for me next semester – I'll have to work hard to find some interesting points. What helped you to find these ideas?	
HIROKO:	I think that one thing that helped me with this was the reading. I've had to do so much reading this semester just to help me make sense of the lectures. At first I couldn't understand what the lecturers were talking about, <u>so I had to turn to the books and journals</u>. Every night I read for hours, using the lists of references that were given, and I made pages of notes. At breakfast, I read and read my notes again. This habit has helped me to follow the ideas in the lectures, and it's also given me some ideas to use in the tutorials.	Q27
SPIROS:	But I did so much reading anyway – I don't think there's any time left over for anything extra. <u>My reading speed is still quite slow</u>, though I'm much better at dealing with vocabulary than I used to be.	Q28
TEACHER:	What else do you think we could add to the course program to help with this reading problem?	
SPIROS:	There's not really anything because it's my problem. I remember we were given long articles to read. We didn't like that but now I realise that reading those long articles was good preparation for the things I need to read now. Also, in class we regularly had speed-reading tasks to do, and we kept a record of our reading speed, so the teachers were encouraging us to work on that.	
HIROKO:	That's true Spiros, but what we read could have been different. Sometimes in the English class I felt frustrated when I had to read articles about the environment or health or education, because <u>I wanted to concentrate on my own field, but we didn't read anything about engineering</u>. So, I think I wasted some time learning vocabulary I didn't need.	Q29
TEACHER:	But surely the strategies you were taught for dealing with that vocabulary were helpful.	

HIROKO: Yes, but psychologically speaking, <u>I would have felt much better working on reading from my own field</u>. What do you think Spiros?   *Q30*

SPIROS: I agree; that would have helped my confidence too and I would have been more motivated. It was good though that we could work on our own topics when we wrote the research assignments.

TEACHER: Okay, let's move on to writing now …

SECTION 4

Good afternoon everyone. Well, with some of you about to go out on field work it's timely that in this afternoon's session I'll be sharing some ideas about the reasons why groups of whales and dolphins sometimes swim ashore from the sea right onto the beach and, most often, die in what are known as 'mass strandings'.

Unfortunately, this type of event is a frequent occurrence in some of the locations that you'll be travelling to, where sometimes <u>the tide goes out suddenly</u>, confusing the animals. However, there are many other theories about the causes of mass strandings.   *Q31*

The first is that the behaviour is linked to parasites. It's often found that stranded animals were infested with large numbers of parasites. For instance, a type of worm is commonly found in the ears of dead whales. <u>Since marine animals rely heavily on their hearing to navigate, this type of infestation has the potential to be very harmful</u>.   *Q32*

Another theory is related to toxins, or poisons. These have also been found to contribute to the death of many marine animals. <u>Many toxins, as I'm sure you're aware, originate from plants, or animals</u>. The whale ingests these toxins in its normal feeding behaviour but whether these poisons directly or indirectly lead to stranding and death, seems to depend upon the toxin involved.   *Q33*

In 1988, for example, fourteen humpback whales examined after stranding along the beaches of Cape Cod were found to have been poisoned after eating tuna that contained saxitoxin, the same toxin that can be fatal in humans.

Alternatively, it has also been suggested that some animals strand accidentally by following their prey ashore in the confusion of the chase. In 1995 David Thurston monitored pilot whales that beached after following squid ashore. However, this idea does not seem to hold true for the majority of mass strandings because <u>examination of the animals' stomach contents reveal that most had not been feeding as they stranded</u>.   *Q34*

There are also some new theories which link strandings to humans. A growing concern is that loud noises in the ocean cause strandings. <u>Noises such as those caused by military exercises</u> are of particular concern and <u>have been pinpointed as the cause of some strandings of late</u>.   *Q35*

One of these, a mass stranding of whales in 2000 in the Bahamas coincided closely with experiments using a new submarine detection system. There were several factors that made this stranding stand out as different from previous strandings. This led researchers to look for a new cause. For one, <u>all the stranded animals were healthy</u>. In addition, the <u>animals were spread out along 38 kilometres of coast</u>, whereas it's more common for the animals to be found in a group when mass strandings occur.   *Q36* / *Q37*

A final theory is related to group behaviour, and suggests that sea mammals cannot distinguish between sick and healthy leaders and will follow sick leaders, even to an inevitable death. This is a particularly interesting theory since <u>the whales that are thought to be most social</u> – the toothed whales – <u>are the group that strand the most frequently</u>.   *Q38*

The theory is also supported by evidence from a dolphin stranding in 1994. Examination of the dead animals revealed that <u>apart from the leader, all the others had been healthy</u> at the time of their death.   *Q39*

Without one consistent theory however it is very hard for us to do anything about this phenomenon except to assist animals where and when we can. Stranding networks have been established around the world to aid in rescuing animals and collecting samples from those that could not be helped. I recommend <u>John Connor's *Marine Mammals Ashore*</u> as an excellent starting point <u>if you're interested in finding out more about these networks</u>, or establishing one yourself.   *Q40*

TEST 2

SECTION 1

MAN:	Good morning. Can I help you?	
WOMAN:	Yes. I've just been accepted on a course at the university and I'd like to try and arrange accommodation in the <u>hall of residence</u>.	*Example*
MAN:	Yes, certainly. Please sit down. What I'll do is fill in a form with you to find out a little more about your preferences and so forth.	
WOMAN:	Thank you.	
MAN:	So first of all, can I take your name?	
WOMAN:	It's Anu <u>Bhatt</u>.	*Q1*
MAN:	Could you spell your name please?	
WOMAN:	Yes. A-N-U ... B-H-A double T.	
MAN:	Thanks, and could I ask your date of birth?	
WOMAN:	<u>31st March 1972</u>.	*Q2*
MAN:	Thank you. And where are you from?	
WOMAN:	India.	
MAN:	Oh right. And what will you be studying?	
WOMAN:	<u>I'm doing a course in nursing</u>.	*Q3*
MAN:	Right, thank you. And how long would you want to stay in hall, do you think?	
WOMAN:	Well, it'll take three years but <u>I'd only like to stay in hall for two</u>. I'd like to think about living outside for the third year.	*Q4*
MAN:	Fine. And what did you have in mind for catering? Do you want to cook for yourself or have all your meals provided, that's full board?	
WOMAN:	Is there something in between?	
MAN:	Yes. You can just have evening meal provided, which is half board.	
WOMAN:	That's what I'd prefer.	
MAN:	Yes, a lot of students opt for that. Now, with that in mind, do you have any special diet, anything we should know about?	
WOMAN:	Yes, <u>I don't take red meat</u>.	*Q5*
MAN:	No red meat.	

MAN:	Now, thinking about the room itself, we have a number of options. You can have a single study bedroom or you can have a shared one. These are both what we call simple rooms. The other alternative is to opt for a single bedsit which actually has more space and better facilities. There's about £20 a week difference between them.

WOMAN:	Well, actually my grant is quite generous and <u>I think the bedsit sounds the best option</u>.	Q6
MAN:	Lovely. I'll put you down for that and we'll see what availability is like. Now can I ask some other personal details which we like to have on record?	
WOMAN:	Yes, of course.	
MAN:	I wonder if you could let us know what your interests are. This might help us get a closer match for placing you in a particular hall.	
WOMAN:	Ummm. <u>Well, I love the theatre</u>.	Q7
MAN:	Right.	
WOMAN:	And I enjoy sports, particularly badminton.	
MAN:	That's worth knowing. Now, what we finish with on the form is really a list from you of what your priorities are in choosing a hall and we'll do our best to take these into account.	
WOMAN:	Well, the first thing is <u>I'd prefer a hall where there are other mature students</u>, if possible.	Q8
MAN:	Yes, we do have halls which tend to cater for slightly older students.	
WOMAN:	Ummm and <u>I'd prefer to be out of town</u>.	Q9
MAN:	That's actually very good for you because we tend to have more vacancies in out-of-town halls.	
WOMAN:	Lucky!	
MAN:	Yes. Anything else?	
WOMAN:	Well, <u>I would like somewhere with a shared area</u>, a TV room for example, or something like that. It's a good way to socialise.	Q10
MAN:	It certainly is.	
WOMAN:	That's it.	
MAN:	Now, we just need a contact telephone number for you.	
WOMAN:	Sure, I'll just find it. It's double 67549.	
MAN:	Great, so we'll be in contact with you as soon as possible …	

SECTION 2

Hello, I'm delighted to welcome you to our Wildlife Club, and very pleased that you're interested in the countryside and the plants and creatures of this area. I think you'll be surprised at the variety we have here, even though we're not far from London. I'll start by telling you about some of the parks and open spaces nearby.

One very pleasant place is Halland Common. This has been public land for hundreds of years, and what you'll find interesting is that the River Ouse, which flows into the sea eighty kilometres away, has its source in the common. There's an information board about the plants and animals you can see here, and by the way, the common is accessible 24 hours a day.

Then there's <u>Holt Island, which is noted for its great range of trees</u>. In the past willows were grown here commercially for basket-making, and this ancient craft has recently been reintroduced. The island is only <u>open to the public from Friday to Sunday</u>, because it's quite small, and if there were people around every day, much of the wildlife would keep away.

Q11

Q12

From there it's just a short walk across the bridge to Longfield Country Park. <u>Longfield has a modern replica of a farm from over two thousand years ago</u>. Children's activities are often arranged there, like bread-making and face-painting. The park is only open during daylight hours, so bear that in mind if you decide to go there.

Q13

Longfield Park has a programme of activities throughout the year, and to give you a sample, this is what's happening in the next few days. On Monday you can learn about herbs, and how they've been used over the centuries. You'll start with a tour of our herb garden, <u>practise the technique of using them as colour dyes for cloth</u>, and listen to an illustrated talk about their use in cooking and medicine.   **Q14**

Then on Wednesday you can join local experts to discover the variety of insects and birds that appear in the evening. We keep to a small number of people in the group, <u>so if you   **Q15** want to go you'll need to phone the park ranger a few days ahead</u>. There's a small charge, which you should pay when you turn up.

I'm sure you're all keen to help with the practical task of looking after the park, so on Saturday you can join a working party. You'll have a choice of all sorts of activities, from planting hedges to picking up litter, so you'll be able to change from one to another when you feel like it. The rangers will be hard at work all day, but do come and join in, even for just a short while. One thing, though, is to <u>make sure you're wearing something that you   **Q16** don't mind getting dirty or torn</u>.

And finally I'd like to tell you about our new wildlife area, Hinchingbrooke Park, which will be opened to the public next month. This slide doesn't really indicate how big it is, but anyway, you can see the two gates into the park, and the main paths. As you can see, there's a lake in the north west of the park, with <u>a bird hide to the west of it, at the end of a   **Q17** path</u>. So it'll be a nice quiet place for watching the birds on the lake.

Fairly close to where refreshments are available, <u>there's a dog-walking area in the   **Q18** southern part of the park</u>, leading off from the path. And if you just want to sit and relax, you can go to <u>the flower garden; that's the circular area on the map surrounded by paths</u>.   **Q19**

And finally, there's <u>a wooded area in the western section of the park, between two paths</u>.   **Q20**

Okay, that's enough from me, so let's go on to …

SECTION 3

PAM: Hi Jun. As you know, I've asked you here today to discuss the future of our Self-Access Centre. We have to decide what we want to do about this very important resource for our English language students. So, can you tell me what the students think about this?

JUN: Well, from the students' point of view, we would like to keep it. The majority of students say that they enjoy using it because it provides a variation on the classroom routine and <u>they see it as a pretty major   **Q21** component of their course</u>, but we would like to see some improvements to the equipment, particularly the computers; there aren't enough for one each at the moment and we always have to share.

PAM: Well yes, the teachers agree that it is a very valuable resource but one thing we have noticed is that a lot of the students are using it to check their personal emails. We don't want to stop you students using it, but we think the computers should be used as a learning resource, not for emails. <u>Some of us also think that we could benefit a lot more by relocating the   **Q22** Self-Access Centre to the main University library building</u>. How do you think the students would feel about that, Jun?

JUN: Well, the library is big enough to incorporate the Self-Access Centre, but it wouldn't be like a class activity anymore. <u>Our main worry would be not being   **Q23**</u>

138

	able to go to a teacher for advice. I'm sure there would be plenty of things to do but we really need teachers to help us choose the best activities.	
PAM:	Well, there would still be a teacher present and he or she would guide the activities of the students, we wouldn't just leave them to get on with it.	
JUN:	Yes, but I think the students would be much happier keeping the existing set-up; they really like going to the Self-Access Centre with their teacher and staying together as a group to do activities. If we could just improve the resources and facilities, I think it would be fine. Is the cost going to be a problem?	
PAM:	It's not so much the expense that I'm worried about, and we've certainly got room to do it, but it's the problem of timetabling a teacher to be in there outside class hours. If we're going to spend a lot of money on equipment and resources, we really need to make sure that everything is looked after properly. Anyway, let's make some notes to see just what needs doing to improve the Centre.	Q24

PAM:	Now, what about the computers? I think it might be a good idea to install some new models. They would take up a lot less room and so that would increase the work space for text books and so on.	
JUN:	That would be great. It is a bit cramped in there at times.	
PAM:	What about other resources? Do you have a list of things that the students would like to see improved?	
JUN:	Yes, one of the comments that students frequently make is that they find it difficult to find materials that are appropriate for their level, especially reading resources, so I think we need to label them more clearly.	Q25
PAM:	Well that's easy enough, we can get that organised very quickly. In fact I think we should review all of the study resources as some of them are looking a bit out-of-date.	
JUN:	Definitely. The CD section especially needs to be more current. I think we should get some of the ones that go with our latest course books and also make multiple copies.	Q26
PAM:	Good, now I was also thinking about some different materials that we haven't got in there at all. What do you think of the idea of introducing some workbooks? If we break them up into separate pages and laminate them, they'd be a great resource. The students could study the main course book in class and then do follow-up practice in the Self-Access Centre.	Q27
JUN:	That sounds good.	
PAM:	Okay, now finally we need to think about how the room is used. I'll have to talk to the teachers and make sure we can all reach some agreement on a timetable to supervise the centre after class. But we also need to think about security, too. Especially if we're going to invest in some new equipment.	Q28
JUN:	What about putting in an alarm?	Q29
PAM:	Good idea. The other thing I'd like to do is talk to our technicians and see whether we could somehow limit the access to email. I really don't want to see that resource misused.	Q30
JUN:	What about if we agree to only use it before and after class?	
PAM:	Yes, that would be fine. OK, anyway ... that's great for now. We'll discuss it further when we've managed to ...	

SECTION 4

Good morning everyone. Now whether you're going to university to study business or some other subject, many of you will eventually end up working for a company of some kind.

Now, when you first start working somewhere you will realise that the organisation you've joined has certain characteristics. And we often refer to these social characteristics as the culture of the organisation – this includes its unwritten ideas, beliefs, values and things like that. One well known writer has classified company cultures by identifying four major types.

The first type is called the Power Culture, and it's usually found in small organisations.

It's the type of culture that needs a central source of power to be effective, and because control is in the hands of just one or two people there aren't many rules or procedures. Another characteristic is that communication usually takes the form of conversations rather than, say, formal meetings or written memos. Now one of the benefits of this culture is that the organisation has the ability to act quickly, so it responds well to threat, or danger on the one hand, and opportunity on the other.

Q31

Q32

But on the negative side, this type of organisation doesn't always act effectively, because it depends too much on one or two people at the top, and when these people make poor decisions there's no-one else who can influence them.

Q33

And the kind of person who does well in this type of business culture is one who is happy to take risks, and for whom job security is a low priority.

Q34

The next type is known as Role Culture – that's R-O-L-E, not R-O-double L, by the way, and this type is usually found in large companies, which have lots of different levels in them. These organisations usually have separate departments that specialise in things like finance, or sales, or maintenance, or whatever. Each one is co-ordinated at the top by a small group of senior managers, and typically everyone's job is controlled by sets of rules and procedures – for example, there are specific job descriptions, rules for discipline, and so on.

Q35

Q36

What are the benefits of this kind of culture? Well firstly, because it's found in large organisations, its fixed costs, or overheads as they're known, are low in relation to its output, or what it produces. In other words it can achieve economies of scale. And secondly, it is particularly successful in business markets where technical expertise is important. On the other hand, this culture is often very slow to recognise the need for change, and even slower to react. What kind of person does this type of culture suit? Well it suits employees who value security, and who don't particularly want to have responsibility.

Q37
Q38

Q39

Moving on now to Task Cultures – this type is found in organisations that are project-oriented. You usually find it where the market for the company's product is extremely competitive, or where the products themselves have a short life-span. Usually top management delegates the projects, the people and other resources. And once these have been allocated, little day-to-day control is exercised from the top, because this would seem like 'breaking the rules'.

Now one of the major benefits of this culture is that it's flexible. But it does have some major disadvantages too. For instance, it can't produce economies of scale or great depth of expertise. People who like working in groups or teams prefer this type of culture.

Q40

And finally, the fourth category is called the Person Culture …

TEST 3

SECTION 1

MAN:	Greek Island Holidays, can I help you?
WOMAN:	Yes, I hope so. I have a friend who's just come back from Corfu and she's recommended some apartments in Arilas. She thought they might be on your list.
MAN:	Arilas, Arilas, let me see. Can you give me the names?
WOMAN:	Yes, the first's Rose Garden Apartments. I'd like to go with another friend in the last week of October.
MAN:	Well, we've got a lovely studio flat available at that time. I'm sure you'd enjoy the entertainment programme there too, with <u>Greek dancing</u> in the restaurant.
WOMAN:	And the cost for each of us?
MAN:	£219.
WOMAN:	That sounds very reasonable! I'm just jotting down some notes. Now the second one she mentioned was called Blue Bay.
MAN:	Blue Bay? Yes, in fact that's very popular and it has some special features.
WOMAN:	Really?
MAN:	The main attraction is the large swimming pool with salt water.
WOMAN:	Much healthier, I understand.
MAN:	That's right. And <u>it isn't far from the beach, either – only 300 metres</u>, and only around half a kilometre to some shops, so you don't have to be too energetic.
WOMAN:	Is it much more expensive than the first one?
MAN:	Let me just check. I think at the time you want to go it's around £260 – no £275 to be exact.
WOMAN:	Right, I've got that. Now there are just two more apartments to ask you about. Um, I can't read my own writing! Something to do with sun … Sunshine, is it?
MAN:	I think you meant <u>the Sunshade Apartments</u>. They're on a mountainside.
WOMAN:	Any special features?
MAN:	Yes, each room has its own sun terrace and there are shared barbecue facilities.
WOMAN:	Sounds lovely!
MAN:	Yes, it is rather well-equipped. It also provides water sports – it has its own beach. There are facilities for water-skiing.
WOMAN:	Any kite-surfing? My friend's quite keen.
MAN:	Not at the hotel but I'm sure you'll find some in Arilas. There's also satellite TV in the apartments.
WOMAN:	And how much is that one?
MAN:	£490 with two sharing.
WOMAN:	You mean £245 each?
MAN:	I'm afraid not! Each person has to pay that amount and there must be at least two in an apartment.
WOMAN:	I don't think that would be within our budget, unfortunately. And the last one sounds a bit expensive too – the Grand!

Example

Q1

Q2

MAN:	Actually it's quite reasonable. It's an older style house with Greek paintings in every room, and <u>a balcony</u> outside.	Q3
WOMAN:	Sounds nice. What are the views like?	
MAN:	Well, <u>there are forests all round</u> and they hide a supermarket just down the road, so that's very useful for all your shopping needs. There's a disco in the area too.	Q4
WOMAN:	And the price?	
MAN:	<u>£319 at that time</u>, but if you leave it till November it goes down by 40%.	Q5
WOMAN:	Too late, I'm afraid.	
MAN:	Well, why don't I send you a brochure with full details, Ms … ?	
WOMAN:	Nash. But don't worry about that. I'm coming to Upminster soon and I'll call and get one. I just wanted to get an idea first.	
MAN:	Well, that's fine. We've got plenty here when you come.	

WOMAN:	If you've got a minute, could I just check a couple of points about insurance? I got one policy through the post but I'd like to see if yours is better.	
MAN:	Fine. What would you like to know?	
WOMAN:	Well, the one I've got has benefits and then the maximum amount you can claim. Is that like yours?	
MAN:	Yes, that's how most of them are.	
WOMAN:	Well, the first thing is cancellation. If the holiday's cancelled on the policy I've got, you can claim £8,000.	
MAN:	We can improve on that, Ms Nash. <u>For Greek Island holidays, our maximum is £10,000</u>.	Q6
WOMAN:	That's good – of course our holiday won't even cost £1,000 together!	
MAN:	It's still sensible to have good cover. Now, if you go to hospital, we allow £600.	
WOMAN:	Yes, mine's similar.	
MAN:	And <u>we also allow a relative to travel to your holiday resort</u>.	Q7
WOMAN:	My policy just says their representative will help you.	
MAN:	You can see there's another difference there. And what happens if you don't get on the plane?	
WOMAN:	Nothing, as far as I can see on this form.	
MAN:	Don't you have <u>missed departure</u>?	Q8
WOMAN:	No, I'll just jot that down.	
MAN:	We pay up to £1,000 for that, depending on the reason. And we're particularly generous about loss of personal belongings – up to £3,000, but not more than <u>£500 for a single item</u>.	Q9
WOMAN:	Then I'd better not take my laptop!	
MAN:	Not unless you insure it separately.	
WOMAN:	OK – thanks very much for your time – you've really been helpful. Can I get back to you? Your name is?	
MAN:	<u>Ben – Ludlow. That's L-U-D-L-O-W</u>. I'm the Assistant Manager here. I'll give you my number. It's 081260 543216.	Q10
WOMAN:	But didn't I phone 081260 567294? That's what I've got on the paper.	
MAN:	That's the main switchboard. I've given you my direct line.	
WOMAN:	Right, thank you …	

SECTION 2

WOMAN: For the second in our series about locally-run businesses, we meet Simon Winridge, co-founder of the hugely-successful Winridge Forest Railway Park. Welcome, Simon. Now, perhaps you can begin by telling us a little bit about how it all started.

MAN: Well, during the 1970s, my wife, Liz and I had just acquired 80 acres of sheep-farming land, and we decided to settle down and have children. Pretty soon we had a daughter, Sarah, and a son, Duncan. The place was wonderful for the kids: they particularly loved trains and gradually built up an enormous network of miniature railway track. I began to develop larger-scale models of locomotives but we didn't think anything more of it until I went on a trip to a theme park near Birmingham and decided we could do a much better job! So we set up a small one ourselves based on the miniature railway and we opened to the public for just a month that year, 1984 – in July – our driest month – because our children said they didn't want our guests to have a miserable, wet visit. I dealt with Park business and Liz carried on with the farm work.

It soon became clear that we were onto a winner. We began to extend the railway track and lay it among more interesting landscape by planting trees, which in turn attracted more wildlife, and by making cuttings through the rock.

Nowadays, we're open all year round and we're pleased to say that Winridge is one of the most popular visitor attractions in the area – with 50,000 visitors a year – a million and a half people have been through our doors since we opened.

Q11

Q12

Q13

All these visitors mean we have had to expand our operation and it's now a truly family concern. I'm near to retirement age so I only concern myself with looking after the mechanical side of things – keeping the trains going. Liz now devotes all her energies to recruiting and supporting the large squadron of workers, which keep the place running smoothly. We're really pleased that after some years away teaching, Sarah has now returned to the park and makes sure the visitors are kept fed and watered, which keeps her pretty busy as you can imagine. Our son, Duncan, has been a stalwart of the park for the last ten years, taking over from me in the area of construction – and I'll say a little bit more about that in a moment – and his new wife, Judith, has also joined the team in charge of retail. That's becoming a tremendous growth area for us – a lot of people want to buy souvenirs.

Q14

Q15

Q16

Q17

Q18

WOMAN: So have you finished your development of the site for the moment?

MAN: Not at all! We're constantly looking for ways to offer more to our visitors. The railway remains the central feature and there's now 1.2 kilometres of the line laid but we'd like to lay more. Because of the geology of the area, our greatest problem is digging tunnels. But we're gradually overcoming that. We're also very pleased with a new installation of the Go-Kart arena which is 120 square metres in area. Again the problem is the geology; we had to level the mounds on the track for safety reasons. We wanted to enable 5–12 year olds to use the go-karts. And the main attraction here is the Formula 1 Kart. We've known fights to break out over who gets it! And then finally to our most recent development which is the landscaped …

Q19

Q20

SECTION 3

TUTOR:	Ah Caroline … come on in. Sit down.
CAROLINE:	Thanks.
TUTOR:	So how's the dissertation planning going?
CAROLINE:	Well Dr Schulmann, I'm still having a lot of trouble deciding on a title.
TUTOR:	Well, that's perfectly normal at this stage. And this is what your tutorials will help you to do.
CAROLINE:	Right.
TUTOR:	What we'll do is jot down some points that might help you in your decision. First of all, you have chosen your general topic area, haven't you?
CAROLINE:	Yes, it's the fishing industry.	Q21
TUTOR:	Oh yes, that was one of the areas you mentioned. Now, what aspects of the course are you good at?
CAROLINE:	Well, I think I'm coping well with statistics, and I'm never bored by it.	Q22
TUTOR:	Good. Anything else?
CAROLINE:	Well, I found computer modelling fascinating – I have no problem following what's being taught, whereas quite a few of my classmates find it difficult.
TUTOR:	Well, that's very good. Do you think these might be areas you could bring into your dissertation?
CAROLINE:	Oh yes, if possible. It's just that I'm having difficulty thinking how I can do that. You see I feel I don't have sufficient background information.
TUTOR:	I see. Well, do you take notes?
CAROLINE:	I'm very weak at note-taking. My teachers always used to say that.	Q23
TUTOR:	Well, I think you really need to work on these weaknesses before you go any further.
CAROLINE:	What do you suggest?

TUTOR:	Well, I can go through the possible strategies with you and let you decide where to go from there.
CAROLINE:	Okay, thanks.
TUTOR:	Well, some people find it helpful to organise peer-group discussions – you know, each week a different person studies a different topic and shares it with the group.
CAROLINE:	Oh right.
TUTOR:	It really helps build confidence, you know, having to present something to others.	Q24
CAROLINE:	I can see that.
TUTOR:	The drawback is that everyone in the group seems to share the same ideas … they keep being repeated in all the dissertations.	Q25
CAROLINE:	Okay.
TUTOR:	You could also try a service called 'Student Support'. It's designed to give you a structured programme over a number of weeks to develop your skills.	Q26
CAROLINE:	Sounds good.
TUTOR:	Yes, unfortunately there are only a few places. But it's worth looking into.	Q27
CAROLINE:	Yes, of course. I know I've got to work on my study skills.
TUTOR:	And then there are several study skills books you can consult.
CAROLINE:	Right.

TUTOR:	They'll be a good source of reference but <u>the problem is they are sometimes too general</u>.	Q28
CAROLINE:	Yes, that's what I've found.	
TUTOR:	Other than that I would strongly advise quite simple ideas like using a card index.	
CAROLINE:	Well, yes, I've never done that before.	
TUTOR:	It's simple, but it really works because you have to get points down in a small space. Another thing I always advise is don't just take your notes and forget about them. <u>Read everything three times</u> – that'll really fix them in your mind.	Q29
CAROLINE:	Yes, I can see it'd take discipline but …	
TUTOR:	Well, if you establish good study skills at this stage they'll be with you all your life.	
CAROLINE:	Oh yes, I completely agree. It's just that I don't seem to be able to discipline myself. I need to talk things over.	
TUTOR:	Well, we'll be continuing these tutorials of course. Let's arrange next month's now. Let's see, I can see you virtually any time during the week starting 22nd January.	
CAROLINE:	What about the 24th? I'm free in the afternoon.	
TUTOR:	Sorry, I'm booked then. What about the following day?	
CAROLINE:	Thursday? I can make the morning.	
TUTOR:	Fine, <u>we'll go for the 25th then</u>.	Q30
CAROLINE:	That's great, thanks.	

SECTION 4

Good morning. In the last few lectures I've been talking about the history of domestic building construction. But today I want to begin looking at some contemporary, experimental designs for housing. So, I'm going to start with a house which is constructed more or less under the ground. And one of the interesting things about this project is that the owners – both professionals but not architects – wanted to be closely involved, so they decided to manage the project themselves. <u>Their chief aim was to create somewhere that was as environmentally-friendly as possible</u>. But at the same time they wanted to live somewhere peaceful – they'd both grown up in a rural area and disliked urban life.   Q31

So the first thing they did was to look for a site. And they found a disused stone quarry in a beautiful area. <u>The price was relatively low</u>, and they liked the idea of recycling the land, as it were. As it was, the quarry was an ugly blot on the landscape, and it wasn't productive any longer, either.   Q32

They consulted various architects and looked at a number of designs before finally deciding on one. As I've said, it was a design for a sort of underground house, and it was built into the earth itself, with two storeys. The north, east and west sides were set in the earth, and only the sloping, south-facing side was exposed to light. <u>That was made of a double layer of very strong glass</u>. There were also photovoltaic tiles fixed to the top and bottom of this sloping wall. These are tiles that are designed to store energy from the sun. <u>And the walls had a layer of foam around them too, to increase the insulation</u>.   Q33   Q34

Now, what is of interest to us about this project is the features which make the building energy-efficient. <u>Sunlight floods in through the glass wall, and to maximise it there are lots of mirrors and windows inside the house</u>. That helps to spread the light around. So that's the first thing – light is utilised as fully as possible.   Q35

In addition, the special tiles on the outside convert energy from the sun and generate some of the house's electricity. In fact, and <u>it's possible that in future the house may even generate an electricity surplus</u>, and that the owners will be able to sell some to the national grid. *Q36*

As well as that, wherever possible, recycled materials have been used. For example, <u>the floors are made of reclaimed wood</u>. And the owners haven't bought a single item of new furniture – they just kept what they already had. And then there's <u>the system for dealing with the waste produced in the house. This is dealt with organically</u> – it's purified by being filtered through reed beds which have been planted for that purpose in the garden. So the occupants of the house won't pollute the land or use any damaging chemicals. *Q37* *Q38*

<u>It's true that the actual construction of the house was harmful to the environment, mainly because they had to use massive amounts of concrete</u> – one of the biggest sources of carbon dioxide in manufacturing. And, as you know, this is very damaging to the environment. In total, the house construction has released 70 tons of carbon dioxide into the air. Now that's a frightening thought. However, <u>once the initial 'debt' has been cleared – and it's been calculated that this will only take fifteen years</u> – this underground house won't cost anything – environmentally I mean – because unlike ordinary houses, it is run in a way that is completely environmentally friendly. *Q39* *Q40*

So, eco-housing like this is likely to become much more …

TEST 4

SECTION 1

WOMAN:	Can I help you?
MAN:	Yes, I've just moved to this area with my wife and children and I'd like to know where we can all register with a doctor at a Health Centre.
WOMAN:	Okay. Well, there's <u>Doctor Green</u> at The Harvey Clinic. <u>We always recommend her for babies</u>, because she's very good with them and she runs a special clinic.
MAN:	Oh … actually my youngest child is five, so that wouldn't be any good for us.
WOMAN:	Right.
MAN:	Is there anywhere else I could try?
WOMAN:	Yes, the <u>Eshcol</u> Health Practice is the next one on my list.
MAN:	How do you spell that?
WOMAN:	E-S-H-C-O-L. And it's Doctor Fuller, who has space on his list. The clinic only opened a year ago, so the facilities are all very modern.
MAN:	That sounds good.
WOMAN:	And it's particularly good if you're busy during the day, because <u>they also do appointments in the evening</u>. They're closed on Saturday, though. The only other place on the list is the Health Centre on Shore Lane. You can register with Doctor <u>Gormley</u>, that's G-O-R-M-L-E-Y. He's new there, but the centre has a very good reputation.
MAN:	Oh yes, I think I know the road. That would be the best one. Thanks. Could you tell me, will all their services be free?

Example *Q1*

Q2

Q3

Q4

WOMAN:	Erm … there are usually some small charges that doctors make. Let me see what it says about the Shore Lane Centre. <u>If you need to be vaccinated before any trips abroad, you won't have to pay for this</u>. Erm, what else? The sports injury treatment service operates on a paying basis, as does the nutritional therapy service. Some health centres do offer alternative therapies like homeopathy as part of their pay-to-use service. Shore Lane are hoping to do this soon – I think they may start with acupuncture. And finally, <u>if you need to prove you're healthy or haven't had any serious injuries before a new employer will accept you, you can get a free fitness check-up there</u>, but you'd most likely have to pay for insurance medicals though.	*Q5 & 6* *Q5 & 6*
MAN:	Okay, thanks.	

WOMAN:	You might also be interested to know the Centre is running a pilot scheme of talks for patients. I've got the list here. Actually, they look very interesting.	
MAN:	What sort of things?	
WOMAN:	Well, the first one's about giving up smoking. It's next week, the twenty-fifth of February, at 7 pm, and that's in Room 4. It says, <u>the talk will stress the health benefits particularly for people with asthma or heart disease</u>.	*Q7*
MAN:	That sounds very interesting.	
WOMAN:	There's also a talk for families with children. It's on Healthy Eating, and takes place on the first of March at five o'clock.	
MAN:	Will that be at the Health Centre?	
WOMAN:	Erm, actually <u>it's at the primary school on Shore Lane</u>. I imagine they're inviting the parents of pupils there – it says here 'all welcome'.	*Q8*
MAN:	Mmm, I might go to that if I have time.	
WOMAN:	There's a couple of other talks – one giving advice about how to avoid injuries while doing exercise. It's on the ninth of March. Oh, it's a late afternoon talk, at <u>four thirty</u>, and it'll be in Room 6. It also says the talk is <u>suitable for all ages</u>. And finally, there's a talk called 'Stress Management' which is …	*Q9* *Q10*

SECTION 2

MAN:	Hello?
WOMAN:	Hi. It's Laura Carlton here. We've just arrived at the holiday flat, but I can't get the hot water and heating to work.
MAN:	Oh right! That's easy. Don't worry. In the upstairs cupboard, you'll find the water heater. You'll see three main controls on the left at the bottom of the heater. <u>The first one – the round one on the far left – is the most important one for the heating and hot water. It's the main control switch</u>. Make sure it's in the 'on' position. The switch itself doesn't light up, but the little square below will be black if the switch is 'off'. That's probably what's happened – it's got switched off by mistake. The middle one of these three controls – you'll see it's slightly larger than the first one – controls the radiators. If you feel cold while you're there and need the radiators on, this needs to be turned to maximum. The last of the three controls – the one on the right – is usually on about a number four setting which for the water in the taps is usually quite hot enough.

Q11 (aligned to "The first one – the round one on the far left – is the most")

	Below the heating controls in the middle is a small round plastic button. If	*Q12*
	there isn't enough water in the pipes, sometimes the heater goes out. If	
	this happens you'll need to press this button to reset the heater. Hold it in	*Q12*
	for about five seconds and the heater should come on again. Then there's	
	a little square indicator under the third knob that's a kind of alarm light. It'll	*Q13*
	flash if you need to reset the heater.	

WOMAN: It sounds complicated ...

MAN: I'm sure you won't have any problems with it. There should be some more instructions on the side of the heater. Call me back if you can't make it work.

WOMAN: Okay.

WOMAN: While you're on the phone, we haven't managed to find a few things we need, like extra pillows for the beds and some washing powder. Is there any here?

MAN: Pillows ... yes. If you look in the cupboard, the large white one upstairs – *Q14*
to the left of the bathroom door – there should be four or five on the top
shelf. And if you want to do some washing, there's some powder for that
... probably by the back door. There's a kind of shelf there above the sink. *Q15*
In fact, I'm sure there's some there, in a large blue box. You need about
half a cup full for each wash.

And that reminds me, the spare key to the back door is hanging on a hook *Q16*
on the wall by the sitting room window. Please make sure to put it back
when you've used it. The previous guests lost it in the garden and I had to
get another one made! And if you have any trouble with the lamps, you'll
find some spare bulbs in a large cardboard box. It's on top of the washing *Q17*
machine with all kinds of useful things in it.

Oh, and another thing I forgot to mention when we last spoke ...

WOMAN: Yes?

MAN: I've left you a local map, so you'll be able to find your way around easily. It *Q18*
shows the whole area. I put it in the top drawer of the chest under the TV
in your bedroom. There's a whole file of local information in there too.

WOMAN: Thanks. What about visiting the town? Can you give us any advice?

MAN: Yes. You'll need to take the car. It's too far to walk from the flat really. You
have to pay to leave your car in all the car parks now I'm afraid ... I like the
one that's by the station best and you can walk to the town centre from
there in five minutes. That's where all the best restaurants are. But if you
want a takeaway, the Italian one does really good pasta and pizzas. Call *Q19*
7-3 double 2, 8-1 for that one, or 7 double 6, double 1, 9 for the Chinese.
They're both good and they'll both deliver to the flat.

As for places to visit, yes, do go and see the railway museum. The
exhibition is small but really good. It gets very crowded on Sundays,
so I suggest you visit it on a quieter day, later in the week, but not on *Q20*
Thursdays which is market day – you won't find anywhere to park and it's
also the only day of the week when they're not open! Anything else?

WOMAN: Not for the moment. Thanks!

SECTION 3

PAUL:	Hello, Kira, how are you?
KIRA:	Fine thanks, Paul, how are you?
PAUL:	Well, thanks. It's good to see you. It must be twelve months since you did our course?
KIRA:	That's right. It's nice to come back and say hello.
PAUL:	What course did you enrol in?
KIRA:	Actually, I went straight into third year Pharmacy. They credited me with two years, which probably made it more difficult for me.
PAUL:	On the other hand, you were lucky to be granted credits. Is that why you chose the course?
KIRA:	Yes. And, as <u>I'd already finished a course in it in my country,</u> I thought it would be easier if I studied something I already knew.
PAUL:	I didn't realise you went into third year. I thought you started in first year. No wonder it was so hard! And what do you think is one of the big differences between studying at a university here and studying in your country?
KIRA:	Well, I've found it very difficult to write assignments, because I wasn't familiar with that aspect of the system here. The main problem is that the lecturers expect you to be critical. That made me feel really terrible. I thought "How can I possibly do it? How can I comment on someone else's research when they probably spent five years doing it?" I think a lot of people who come from overseas countries have similar problems. But after a while it became easier for me. People expect you to have problems with the process of reading and writing but, in fact, <u>it is more a question of altering your viewpoint towards academic study</u>.
PAUL:	How was the content of the lectures? Was it easy for you?
KIRA:	I didn't really have many problems understanding lectures. The content was very similar to what I'd studied before.
PAUL:	And what about the lecturers themselves? Are they essentially the same as lecturers in your country?
KIRA:	Well actually, no. <u>Here, they're much easier to approach</u>. After every lecture you can go and ask them something you didn't understand. Or you can make an appointment and talk to them about anything in the course.
PAUL:	Maybe you found them different because <u>you're a more mature student now</u>, whereas when you were studying in your country you were younger and not so assertive.
KIRA:	No, I don't think that's the difference. Most of the students here do it. In my faculty, they all seem to make appointments – usually to talk about something in the course that's worrying them, but <u>sometimes just about something that might really interest them</u>, something they might want to specialise in. The lecturers must set aside certain times every week when they're available for students.
PAUL:	That's good to hear.

PAUL:	And how was your timetable? Was it a very busy year?
KIRA:	Very, very busy. They make you work very hard. Apart from lectures, we had practical sessions in a lot of subjects. <u>We did these in small groups.</u> I had to go and work four hours every week in a community pharmacy. Actually, I enjoyed this very much – meeting new people all the time. Then

Q21

Q22

Q23

Q24

Q25

Q26

	in second semester, we had to get experience in hospital dispensaries, so <u>every second day we went to one of the big hospitals and worked there</u>.	Q27
	And on top of all that we had our assignments, which took me a lot of time. Oh, I nearly forgot, between first and second semesters, <u>we had to work full-time for two weeks in a hospital</u>.	Q28
PAUL:	That does sound a very heavy year. So are you pleased now that you did it? Do you feel some sense of achievement?	
KIRA:	Yeah, <u>I do feel much more confident</u>, which I suppose is the most important thing.	Q29
PAUL:	And have you got any recommendations for people who are studying from overseas?	
KIRA:	Well, I suppose they need very good English. It would be much better if they spent more time learning English before they enter the university, because you can be in big trouble if you don't understand what people are saying and you haven't got time to translate.	
PAUL:	Anything else?	
KIRA:	Well, as I said before, <u>the biggest problem for me was a lack of familiarity with the education system here</u>.	Q30
PAUL:	It sounds as if it was a real challenge. Congratulations, Kira.	
KIRA:	Thanks, Paul.	

SECTION 4

Good morning. Today I'd like to present the findings of our Year 2 project on wildlife found in gardens throughout our city. I'll start by saying something about the background to the project, then talk a little bit about our research techniques, and then indicate some of our interim findings.

First of all, how did we choose our topic? Well, there are four of us in the group and one day while we were discussing a possible focus, <u>two of the group mentioned that they had seen yet more sparrow-hawks – one of Britain's most interesting birds of prey – in their own city centre gardens and wondered why they were turning up in these gardens in great numbers</u>. We were all very engaged by the idea of why wild animals would choose to inhabit a city garden. Why is it so popular with wildlife when the countryside itself is becoming less so?   Q31

The first thing we did was to establish what proportion of the urban land is taken up by private gardens. We estimated that it was about one fifth, and <u>this was endorsed by looking at large-scale usage maps in the town land survey office</u> – 24% to be precise. Our own informal discussions with neighbours and friends led us to believe that many garden owners had interesting experiences to relate regarding wild animal sightings so we decided to <u>survey garden owners from different areas of the city. Just over 100 of them completed a survey once every two weeks for twelve months – ticking off species they had seen from a pro forma list – and adding the names of any rarer ones</u>. Meanwhile, we were doing our own observations in selected gardens throughout the city. <u>We deliberately chose smaller ones because they were by far the most typical in the city. The whole point of the project was to look at the norm not the exception.</u> Alongside this primary research on urban gardens, <u>we were studying a lot of books about the decline of wild animals in the countryside</u> and thinking of possible causes for this.   Q32 Q33 Q34 Q35

So what did we find? Well, so much that I just won't have time to tell you about here. If you're interested in reading our more comprehensive findings, we've produced detailed graphic representations on the college web-site and of course any of the group would be happy to talk to you about them. Just email us.

What we've decided to present today is information about just three species – because we felt these gave a good indication of the processes at work in rural and urban settings as a whole.   *Q36*

The first species to generate a lot of interesting information was frogs. And there was a clear pattern here – they proliferate where there is suitable water. Garden ponds are on the increase, rural ponds are disappearing, leading to massive migration to the towns.   *Q37*

Hedgehogs are also finding it easier to live in urban areas – this time because their predators are not finding it quite so attractive to leave their rural environment, so hedgehogs have a better survival rate in cities. We had lots of sightings, so all in all we had no difficulties with our efforts to count their numbers precisely.   *Q38*

     Q39

Our final species is the finest of bird singers, the song thrush. On the decline in the countryside, they are experiencing a resurgence in urban gardens because these days gardeners are buying lots of different plants which means there's an extensive range of seeds around, which is what they feed on. Another factor is the provision of nesting places – which is actually better in gardens than the countryside. Hard to believe it, but it's true. Incidentally, we discovered that a massive new survey on song thrushes is about to be launched, so you should keep an eye open for that.   *Q40*

Now, I'd be happy to answer any questions you may have …

Listening and Reading Answer Keys

TEST 1

LISTENING

Section 1, Questions 1–10

1	answer(ing) (the) phone
2	Hillsdunne Road
3	library
4	4.45
5	national holidays
6	after 11 (o'clock)
7	clear voice
8	think quickly
9	22 October
10	Manuja

Section 2, Questions 11–20

11	branch
12	west
13	clothing
14	10
15	running
16	bags
17	A
18	A
19&20	*IN EITHER ORDER*
	A
	E

Section 3, Questions 21–30

21	B
22	C
23	B
24	A
25	C
26	B
27	A
28	B
29	C
30	B

Section 4, Questions 31–40

31	tide/tides
32	hearing/ear/ears
33	*IN EITHER ORDER; BOTH REQUIRED FOR ONE MARK*
	plants
	animals/fish/fishes
34	feeding
35	noise/noises
36	healthy
37	group
38	social
39	leader
40	network/networks

If you score...

0–12	13–29	30–40
you are unlikely to get an acceptable score under examination conditions and we recommend that you spend a lot of time improving your English before you take IELTS.	you may get an acceptable score under examination conditions but we recommend that you think about having more practice or lessons before you take IELTS.	you are likely to get an acceptable score under examination conditions but remember that different institutions will find different scores acceptable.

ACADEMIC READING

Reading Passage 1, Questions 1–13

1	FALSE
2	NOT GIVEN
3	FALSE
4	TRUE
5	NOT GIVEN
6	TRUE
7	NOT GIVEN
8	(the / only) rich
9	commercial (possibilities)
10	mauve (was/is)
11	(Robert) Pullar
12	(in) France
13	malaria (is)

Reading Passage 2, Questions 14–26

14	iv
15	vii
16	i
17	ii
18	several billion years
19	radio (waves/signals)
20	1000 (stars)
21	YES
22	YES
23	NOT GIVEN
24	NO
25	NOT GIVEN
26	NO

Reading Passage 3, Questions 27–40

27	plants
28	*IN EITHER ORDER; BOTH REQUIRED FOR ONE MARK* breathing reproduction
29	gills
30	dolphins
31	NOT GIVEN
32	FALSE
33	TRUE
34	3 measurements
35	(triangular) graph
36	cluster
37	amphibious
38	half way
39	dry-land tortoises
40	D

If you score...

0–11	12–27	28–40
you are unlikely to get an acceptable score under examination conditions and we recommend that you spend a lot of time improving your English before you take IELTS.	you may get an acceptable score under examination conditions but we recommend that you think about having more practice or lessons before you take IELTS.	you are likely to get an acceptable score under examination conditions but remember that different institutions will find different scores acceptable.

TEST 2

LISTENING

Section 1, Questions 1–10

1 Bhatt
2 31 March
3 nursing
4 2
5 meat
6 bedsit
7 theatre/theater
8 mature/older
9 town
10 shared

Section 2, Questions 11–20

11 trees
12 Friday/Sunday
13 farm
14 C
15 B
16 A
17 A
18 I
19 F
20 E

Section 3, Questions 21–30

21 C
22 B
23 B
24 C
25 reading
26 CD
27 workbooks
28 timetable/schedule
29 alarm
30 email/emails

Section 4, Questions 31–40

31 central
32 conversation/conversations
33 effectively
34 risk/risks
35 levels
36 description/descriptions
37 technical
38 change
39 responsibility
40 flexible

If you score...

0–12	13–29	30–40
you are unlikely to get an acceptable score under examination conditions and we recommend that you spend a lot of time improving your English before you take IELTS.	you may get an acceptable score under examination conditions but we recommend that you think about having more practice or lessons before you take IELTS.	you are likely to get an acceptable score under examination conditions but remember that different institutions will find different scores acceptable.

ACADEMIC READING

Reading Passage 1, Questions 1–13

1	H
2	C
3	B
4	I
5	D
6	A
7	two decades
8	crowd (noise)
9	invisible (disabilities/disability)
10	Objective 3

11&12   *IN EITHER ORDER*
   A
   C
| 13 | C |

Reading Passage 2, Questions 14–26

14	F
15	D
16	G
17	E
18	D
19	A
20	B
21	C
22	FALSE
23	FALSE
24	TRUE
25	NOT GIVEN
26	TRUE

Reading Passage 3, Questions 27–40

27	C
28	B
29	D
30	C
31	B
32	YES
33	YES
34	NOT GIVEN
35	NO
36	NOT GIVEN
37	NO
38	A
39	B
40	C

If you score...

0–11	12–28	29–40
you are unlikely to get an acceptable score under examination conditions and we recommend that you spend a lot of time improving your English before you take IELTS.	you may get an acceptable score under examination conditions but we recommend that you think about having more practice or lessons before you take IELTS.	you are likely to get an acceptable score under examination conditions but remember that different institutions will find different scores acceptable.

Listening and Reading Answer Keys

TEST 3

LISTENING

Section 1, Questions 1–10

1	300
2	Sunshade
3	balcony
4	forest/forests
5	319
6	10,000
7	relative
8	missed
9	item
10	Ludlow

Section 2, Questions 11–20

11	C
12	A
13	C
14	E
15	H
16	F
17	C
18	G
19	120
20	5 to 12

Section 3, Questions 21–30

21	fishing industry
22	statistics
23	note-taking
24	confidence
25	ideas
26	student support
27	places
28	general
29	3 times
30	25

Section 4, Questions 31–40

31	B
32	A
33	glass
34	insulation
35	windows
36	electricity
37	floor/floors
38	waste
39	concrete
40	15 years

If you score…

0–12	13–28	29–40
you are unlikely to get an acceptable score under examination conditions and we recommend that you spend a lot of time improving your English before you take IELTS.	you may get an acceptable score under examination conditions but we recommend that you think about having more practice or lessons before you take IELTS.	you are likely to get an acceptable score under examination conditions but remember that different institutions will find different scores acceptable.

ACADEMIC READING

Reading Passage 1, Questions 1–13

1	YES
2	NO
3	YES
4	NOT GIVEN
5	YES
6	YES
7	NO
8	YES
9	H
10	F
11	A
12	C
13	B

Reading Passage 2, Questions 14–26

14	C
15	E
16	A
17	C

18–22 *IN ANY ORDER*

A
D
E
F
J

23	maintenance
24	slow (turning)
25	low pressure
26	cavitation

Reading Passage 3, Questions 27–40

27	D
28	F
29	B
30	E
31	A
32	C

33 *IN EITHER ORDER; BOTH REQUIRED FOR ONE MARK*

Jupiter
Saturn

34 Solar System

35 *IN EITHER ORDER; BOTH REQUIRED FOR ONE MARK*

sensors
circuits

36	spares
37	radio dish
38	TRUE
39	TRUE
40	FALSE

If you score...

0–12	13–29	30–40
you are unlikely to get an acceptable score under examination conditions and we recommend that you spend a lot of time improving your English before you take IELTS.	you may get an acceptable score under examination conditions but we recommend that you think about having more practice or lessons before you take IELTS.	you are likely to get an acceptable score under examination conditions but remember that different institutions will find different scores acceptable.

TEST 4

LISTENING

Section 1, Questions 1–10

1 babies
2 Eshcol
3 evening
4 Gormley
5&6 *IN EITHER ORDER*
    B
    E
7 heart
8 primary school
9 4.30
10 ages

Section 2, Questions 11–20

11 B
12 C
13 E
14 B
15 E
16 D
17 A
18 C
19 732281
20 Thursday/Thursdays

Section 3, Questions 21–30

21 A
22 C
23 approach
24 mature
25 interest
26 groups
27 every 2 days
28 2 weeks
29 confident
30 education system

Section 4, Questions 31–40

31 C
32 A
33 B
34 B
35 A
36 C
37 frog/frogs
38 predators
39 count
40 seed/seeds

If you score...

0–12	13–29	30–40
you are unlikely to get an acceptable score under examination conditions and we recommend that you spend a lot of time improving your English before you take IELTS.	you may get an acceptable score under examination conditions but we recommend that you think about having more practice or lessons before you take IELTS.	you are likely to get an acceptable score under examination conditions but remember that different institutions will find different scores acceptable.

ACADEMIC READING

Reading Passage 1, Questions 1–13

1	FALSE
2	NOT GIVEN
3	TRUE
4	FALSE
5	TRUE
6	NOT GIVEN
7	thorium
8	pitchblende
9	radium
10	soldiers
11	illness
12	neutron
13	leukaemia/leukemia

Reading Passage 2, Questions 14–26

14	G
15	C
16	G
17	D
18	H
19	E
20	D
21	B
22	E
23	C
24	mirror
25	communication
26	ownership

Reading Passage 3, Questions 27–40

27	ii
28	vi
29	i
30	iii
31	B
32	A
33	D
34	D
35	C
36	B
37	FALSE
38	NOT GIVEN
39	FALSE
40	TRUE

If you score...

0–11	12–28	29–40
you are unlikely to get an acceptable score under examination conditions and we recommend that you spend a lot of time improving your English before you take IELTS.	you may get an acceptable score under examination conditions but we recommend that you think about having more practice or lessons before you take IELTS.	you are likely to get an acceptable score under examination conditions but remember that different institutions will find different scores acceptable.

GENERAL TRAINING TEST A

Section 1, Questions 1–14

1 D
2 C
3 A
4 G
5 F
6 B
7 F
8 C
9 G
10 B
11 A
12 A
13 E
14 D

Section 2, Questions 15–27

15 professional image
16 pressed
17 tasteful
18 allergic reactions
19 cultural tradition
20 company logo
21 verbal warning
22 progress
23 five years
24 (residential) clubs
25 concerts
26 leisure skills
27 loan

Section 3, Questions 28–40

28 C
29 B
30 G
31 F
32 E
33 H
34 August 31st
35 human chain/chains
36 blotting paper
37 (countless) dustbins
38 C
39 C
40 D

If you score...

0–19	20–32	33–40
you are unlikely to get an acceptable score under examination conditions and we recommend that you spend a lot of time improving your English before you take IELTS.	you may get an acceptable score under examination conditions but we recommend that you think about having more practice or lessons before you take IELTS.	you are likely to get an acceptable score under examination conditions but remember that different institutions will find different scores acceptable.

GENERAL TRAINING TEST B

Section 1, Questions 1–14

1 full-time education
2 (officially) stamped
3 minimum fares
4 signature
5 anybody else
6 purchase facilities
7 full fare/rate
8 25 per cent/%
9 Sales Department
10 15 per cent/%
11 10 per cent/%
12 same day returns
13 **IN EITHER ORDER; BOTH REQUIRED FOR ONE MARK**
    dates
    times
14 2 minutes

Section 2, Questions 15–27

15 trade certificates
16 (formal) education
17 salary (level)
18 apprenticeship (training)
19 (job) interviews
20 (workforce/workplace) diversity
21 compliment
22 sentence
23 story
24 props
25 time
26 game
27 confidence

Section 3, Questions 28–40

28 A
29 D
30 B
31 commercial
32 miniature
33 wings
34 300 kph
35 skydiver
36 D
37 A
38 D
39 C
40 B

If you score...

0–19	20–31	32–40
you are unlikely to get an acceptable score under examination conditions and we recommend that you spend a lot of time improving your English before you take IELTS.	you may get an acceptable score under examination conditions but we recommend that you think about having more practice or lessons before you take IELTS.	you are likely to get an acceptable score under examination conditions but remember that different institutions will find different scores acceptable.

Model and sample answers for Writing tasks

TEST 1, WRITING TASK 1

SAMPLE ANSWER

This is an answer written by a candidate who achieved a **Band 7** score. Here is the examiner's comment:

> This answer clearly presents the key features of the diagrams, and although the first map is described only briefly, this is acceptable for this particular task. The description is accurate though some aspects, such as the section on the accommodation, could have been more fully extended. The final paragraph summarises the main points effectively. The information is logically organised and can be easily followed throughout the response. A range of cohesive devices including reference and substitution is used appropriately, with only occasional inaccuracies. Some less common vocabulary and collocations are used appropriately, e.g. *central reception block*; *western accommodation units*, and there are no spelling errors. There is a variety of grammatical structures and many sentences contain no inaccuracies. Where errors do occur, they do not affect understanding.

The two maps show the same island while first one is before and the second one is after the construction for tourism.

Looking first at the one before construction, we can see a huge island with a beach in the west. The total length of the island is approximately 250 metres.

Moving on to the second map, we can see that there are lots of buildings on the island. There are two areas of accommodation. One is in the west near the beach while the other one is in the centre of the island. Between them, there is a restaurant in the north and a central reception block, which is surrounded by a vehicle track. This track also goes down to the pier where people can go sailing in the south sea of the island. Furthermore, tourists can swim near the beach in the west. A footpath connecting the western accommodation units also leads to the beach.

Overall, comparing the two maps, there are significant changes after this development. Not only lots of facilities are built on the island, but also the sea is used for activities. The new island has become a good place for tourism.

TEST 1, WRITING TASK 2

Introduce them earlier
earlier is   educationalists

MODEL ANSWER

This model has been prepared by an examiner as an example of a very good answer. However, please note that this is just one example out of many possible approaches.

Traditionally, children have begun studying foreign languages at secondary school, but introducing them earlier is recommended by some educationalists. This policy has been adopted by some educational authorities or individual schools, with both positive and negative outcomes.

The obvious argument in its favour is that young children pick up languages much more easily than teenagers. Their brains are still programmed to acquire their mother tongue, which facilitates learning another language, and unlike adolescents, they are not inhibited by self-consciousness.

The greater flexibility of the primary timetable allows for more frequent, shorter sessions and for a play-centred approach, thus maintaining learners' enthusiasm and progress. Their command of the language in later life will benefit from this early exposure, while learning other languages subsequently will be easier for them. They may also gain a better understanding of other cultures.

There are, however, some disadvantages. Primary school teachers are generalists, and may not have the necessary language skills themselves. If specialists have to be brought in to deliver these sessions, the flexibility referred to above is diminished. If primary language teaching is not standardised, secondary schools could be faced with a great variety of levels in different languages within their intake, resulting in a classroom experience which undoes the earlier gains. There is no advantage if enthusiastic primary pupils become demotivated as soon as they change schools. However, these issues can be addressed strategically within the policy adopted.

Anything which encourages language learning benefits society culturally and economically, and early exposure to language learning contributes to this. Young children's innate abilities should be harnessed to make these benefits more achievable.

TEST 2, WRITING TASK 1

MODEL ANSWER

This model has been prepared by an examiner as an example of a very good answer. However, please note that this is just one example out of many possible approaches.

The chart shows the time spent by UK residents on different types of telephone calls between 1995 and 2002.

Local fixed line calls were the highest throughout the period, rising from 72 billion minutes in 1995 to just under 90 billion in 1998. After peaking at 90 billion the following year, these calls had fallen back to the 1995 figure by 2002.

National and international fixed line calls grew steadily from 38 billion to 61 billion at the end of the period in question, though the growth slowed over the last two years.

There was a dramatic increase in mobile calls from 2 billion to 46 billion minutes. This rise was particularly noticeable between 1999 and 2002, during which time the use of mobile phones tripled.

To sum up, although local fixed line calls were still the most popular in 2002, the gap between the three categories had narrowed considerably over the second half of the period in question.

TEST 2, WRITING TASK 2

SAMPLE ANSWER

This is an answer written by a candidate who achieved a **Band 8** score. Here is the examiner's comment:

> The answer addresses all parts of the prompt sufficiently, focusing on the benefits for students rather than society. A number of relevant, extended and supported ideas are used to produce a well-developed response to the question. However, some ideas, for example the reference to the crime level, are not fully extended. The ideas are logically ordered and cohesion is consistently well managed. Paragraphing is used appropriately, and progression between paragraphs is managed with some sophistication. A wide range of vocabulary is used to articulate meanings precisely, with skilful use of uncommon lexis, and very few inappropriacies. The range of grammatical structures used is also wide, with only occasional minor errors.

It has been suggested that high school students should be involved in unpaid community services as a compulsory part of high school programmes. Most of the colleges are already providing opportunities to gain work experience, however these are not compulsory. In my opinion, sending students to work in community services is a good idea as it can provide them with many lots of valuable skills.

Life skills are very important and by doing voluntary work, students can learn how to communicate with others and work in a team but also how to manage their time and improve their organisational skills. Nowadays, unfortunately, teenagers do not have many after-school activities. After-school clubs are no longer that popular and students mostly go home and sit in front of the TV, browse internet or play video games.

By giving them compulsory work activities with charitable or community organisations, they will be encouraged to do something more creative. Skills gained through compulsory work will not only be an asset on their CV but also increase their employability. Students will also gain more respect towards work and money as they will realise that it is not that easy to earn them and hopefully will learn to spend them in a more practical way.

Healthy life balance and exercise are strongly promoted by the NHS, and therefore any kind of spare time charity work will prevent from sitting and doing nothing. It could also possibly reduce the crime level in the high school age group. If students have activities to do, they will not be bored and come up with silly ideas which can be dangerous for them or their surroundings.

In conclusion, I think this is a very good idea, and I hope this programme will be put into action for high schools/colleges shortly.

TEST 3, WRITING TASK 1

SAMPLE ANSWER

This is an answer written by a candidate who achieved a **Band 6** score. Here is the examiner's comment:

> The answer addresses the task, reporting sufficient details for the reader to be accurately informed, even though in each chart one element is implied rather than overtly stated. Clear comparisons are drawn between the two countries. An overview is given, although focusing on only one age group reduces its clarity. The information is well organised and a range of linking devices used, e.g. *whereas*; *the latter country*. Vocabulary is adequate for the task and generally accurate, though attempts to use less common words are less successful. A few errors occur in word formation, e.g. *statistic* (statistical); *estimative* (estimate), but they do not affect understanding. Simple and complex sentence forms are produced with few grammatical errors, but the range of structures is rather restricted.

The diagrams show statistic information regarding the ages of the habitants of Yemen and Italy in 2000 and also a estimative for 2050.

We can see that in 2000 the majority of people in Yemen was between 0 and 14 years old, whith 50.1%, whereas in Italy most of the population was between 15-59 years old (61.6%), in the same year. On the other hand, just 3.6% of people in the former country was 60 years old or more in 2000, while in the latter country this figure is represented with 24.1%.

The projections for 2050 show that the number of people with 15-59 years and 60 years or more will increase in Yemen, reaching 57.3% and 5.7% respectively. In contrast, in Italy, the population with 15-59 years will decrease to 46.2%, while people with 60 years or more will grow to 42.3%

Overall, it is possible to see that there is an upward trend on the rates of people with 60 years or more in both countries.

TEST 3, WRITING TASK 2

MODEL ANSWER

This model has been prepared by an examiner as an example of a very good answer.
However, please note that this is just one example out of many possible approaches.

A problem of modern societies is the declining level of health in the general population, with conflicting views on how to tackle this worrying trend. One possible solution is to provide more sports facilities to encourage a more active lifestyle.

Advocates of this believe that today's sedentary lifestyle and stressful working conditions mean that physical activity is no longer part of either our work or our leisure time. If there were easy-to-reach local sports centres, we would be more likely to make exercise a regular part of our lives, rather than just collapsing in front of a screen every evening. The variety of sports that could be offered would cater for all ages, levels of fitness and interests: those with painful memories of PE at school might be happier in the swimming pool than on the football pitch.

However, there may be better ways of tackling this problem. Interest in sport is not universal, and additional facilities might simply attract the already fit, not those who most need them. Physical activity could be encouraged relatively cheaply, for example by installing exercise equipment in parks, as my local council has done. This has the added benefit that parents and children often use them together just for fun, which develops a positive attitude to exercise at an early age.

As well as physical activity, high tax penalties could be imposed on high-fat food products, tobacco and alcohol, as excessive consumption of any of these contributes to poor health. Even improving public transport would help: it takes longer to walk to the bus stop than to the car.

In my opinion, focusing on sports facilities is too narrow an approach and would not have the desired results. People should be encouraged not only to be more physically active but also to adopt a healthier lifestyle in general.

TEST 4, WRITING TASK 1

MODEL ANSWER

This model has been prepared by an examiner as an example of a very good answer. However, please note that this is just one example out of many possible approaches.

> The graph shows energy consumption in the US from 1980 to 2012, and projected consumption to 2030.
>
> Petrol and oil are the dominant fuel sources throughout this period, with 35 quadrillion (35q) units used in 1980, rising to 42q in 2012. Despite some initial fluctuation, from 1995 there was a steady increase. This is expected to continue, reaching 47q in 2030.
>
> Consumption of energy derived from natural gas and coal is similar over the period. From 20q and 15q respectively in 1980, gas showed an initial fall and coal a gradual increase, with the two fuels equal between 1985 and 1990. Consumption has fluctuated since 1990 but both now provide 24q. Coal is predicted to increase steadily to 31q in 2030, whereas after 2014, gas will remain stable at 25q.
>
> In 1980, energy from nuclear, hydro- and solar/wind power was equal at only 4q. Nuclear has risen by 3q, and solar/wind by 2. After slight increases, hydropower has fallen back to the 1980 figure. It is expected to maintain this level until 2030, while the others should rise slightly after 2025.
>
> Overall, the US will continue to rely on fossil fuels, with sustainable and nuclear energy sources remaining relatively insignificant.

TEST 4, WRITING TASK 2

SAMPLE ANSWER

This is an answer written by a candidate who achieved a **Band 4** score. Here is the examiner's comment:

> This answer expresses a position on the topic, but the ideas are not always clear because of repetition and a lack of development (the answer is unfinished and underlength). The information is not organised coherently and it is difficult to follow a progression through the answer. Although some linking devices occur, substitution and referencing are not used, and connections between the ideas are unclear. The range of vocabulary is limited and repetitive, and inappropriate word choices, e.g. *small country language*; *invest*, make it difficult for the reader to follow the meaning. There are some attempts to produce complex sentences and some grammatical structures are produced accurately, but frequent errors and omissions in basic sentence formation and in punctuation make the writing difficult to understand.

I agree about this opinion.

Nowadays, several languages die out. I think this situation is right. In the world. already have to much languages minimum 100 languages include small country. But we know just some languages, kind of English, French Japanese, Chinies.

At this moment, we live in the world, So we need frist language in the world. Therefor several languages need to die out.

Also, small country language is almost difficult to learn and not usuful. so we don't need to learn this languages. Even if we learning this languages not using in the world. Just usuful this country And we don't find small language education academy.

So I think small country languages make spend money and time also we need find first language using all of country. This is very important for all country of developing.

After when decide first language our communication will be more easier with another country people. Beside we don't need invest of another language education, and we can invest another part kind of economic and culture developing by decrease education money.

Accordng to this opinion,

TEST A, WRITING TASK 1 (GENERAL TRAINING)

MODEL ANSWER

This model has been prepared by an examiner as an example of a very good answer. However, please note that this is just one example out of many possible approaches.

Dear Jennifer

I am writing to request some unpaid leave next month.

My parents' 60th wedding anniversary is on March 21st, and they are planning to celebrate this significant achievement with all their children and grandchildren. To do this, they have rented a house big enough to accommodate the whole family.

To participate in this special occasion, I would need to be away from work for four days, from Monday 19th to Thursday 23rd. My schedule for that week is relatively light, apart from two meetings with clients. Netta would be able to attend these in my place, as she has had previous dealings with both companies and knows the relevant staff there. I have no other urgent work commitments at that time.

I would be very grateful if you could allow me this time. These few days are very important to my parents and the whole family, and it would be a way to thank them for all the support they have given me.

Best wishes

TEST A, WRITING TASK 2 (GENERAL TRAINING)

SAMPLE ANSWER

This is an answer written by a candidate who achieved a **Band 6** score. Here is the examiner's comment:

> This answer addresses all parts of the task, though the disadvantages of fame are covered more fully than the advantages. Main ideas are relevant, though the answer would be better if they were developed further. The conclusions drawn are at times repetitive. The organisation of ideas is coherent and some are linked effectively, but the openings of paragraphs 2, 3, 4 and 5 show some limitations. Paragraphs 2 and 3 do not develop a central topic well. Vocabulary is adequate for the task, although inappriacies indicate that the range is restricted. However, the errors which occur in word choice and spelling do not prevent meaning being communicated. Simple and complex sentence forms are used, and although a number of inaccuracies are noticeable in structure and punctuation, communication is rarely affected.

Being a celebrity was not always the easiest way of life. Of course besides all the advanteges of being rich, loved and being famous there are many disadvantiges, that we have to take into consideration. So, after all it is a quite hard question, and we cannot give an easy answer.

Let's just think of the celebrities, and try to get a few benefits of being well-known. Some of them had had a very long way until they reached their part of life when they are celebrities.

But if we just look into their everydays, we can say that they have a very good accommodation and lifestyle: they have an income of what everyone is dreaming, they live in huge houses, they can buy all the cars they want.

But as the saying says: money is nothing, even they are rich, their personal life is not always so beautiful as it seems. Let's just remember the famous teenager singer Britney Spears. In the begining she was just like a young girl that everyone wanted to follow. But as time went on, she had some growing personal life problems. She was seen in nightclubs wearing the least dress, once she cut her hair bald, she had alcohol and drug problems. Anyway, being a celebrity is not often easy and beautiful!

Let's just mention the paparazzos. A celebrity cannot go outside his/her house to pick his/her morning newspaper without being photographed. They have to be very careful about their private life, because their fans are following them, and they always have to behehave perfectly! And since no one of us is perfect, their fans are quite often disappointed.

After all, taking into the consideration all the advanteges and disadvantiges, we should say that being a celebrity is not always easy!

TEST B, WRITING TASK 1 (GENERAL TRAINING)

SAMPLE ANSWER

This is an answer written by a candidate who achieved a **Band 5** score. Here is the examiner's comment:

> The answer addresses all the bullet points but does not cover them adequately, either through insufficient information (the second bullet point) or through lack of clarity (the third bullet point). The purpose of the letter is not always clear. Although organising the letter in line with the bullet points provides some logic, linking devices are not effectively used. Reference and substitution occur but are often unclear. The range of vocabulary is limited but just adequate for the task. While there are no spelling errors, inappropriate word choices and faulty word formation require the reader to make some effort to understand the letter. Complex sentences are attempted, but are mainly limited to 'which' clauses. Frequent grammatical errors and faulty punctuation cause the reader some difficulty.

Dear Sir or Madam

On my recently holiday trip which was in thailand for week. I lost my luggage in which I had too many import documents and my gold watch which I bought from Singapore for someone, which costs me $1500 australian Dollar. Fortunately this comes under my travel insurance which I did from your Insurance company. I have all details of this watch including Tax invoice receipt.

It happens when we enjoyed in a hotel. Later on we forget our one of the bag in a local taxi We tried to find it. but all in vain due to shortage of time.

I would like to request you that I want a claim for it. So In future we being your regular customers by paying all premium and instalments.

I will send you all my policies numbers or other thing in your given address.

Thank you

Yours truly customer

TEST B, WRITING TASK 2 (GENERAL TRAINING)

MODEL ANSWER

This model has been prepared by an examiner as an example of a very good answer. However, please note that this is just one example out of many possible approaches.

What's the happiest time in people's lives: youth or old age; school, career or retirement? All of these have been suggested, but teenage years and adulthood both have many supporters.

Those who believe teenagers are the happiest people cite their lack of responsibilities as a significant factor. They are supported financially and emotionally by their parents, and although they may be included in family decisions, they're not ultimately responsible. However, adolescents are on the threshold of adult life: they're old enough to get a part-time job, so they can enjoy their first taste of financial independence, and their future study and career lie ahead.

Away from these serious concerns, young people have an active social life with their friends, often simply by hanging out with them. And of course, there's the excitement of first love and first heartbreak. With all this to experience, teenagers see their parents' lives as boring and stressful.

However, the reverse is also true. Adults see anxious, self-dramatising adolescents, and appreciate the joys of maturity. These may include a contented family life, long-lasting friendships and a career. Long-term relationships may not have the fireworks of adolescence, but are stronger for it, because of the wealth of shared experience. At work, many of us are challenged and stimulated by the increasing professional skills we acquire, which ensures that our jobs remain interesting.

The greatest benefit, though, is that maturity gives you greater confidence in your own judgement, in all areas of life. You're not afraid to express your opinion when others disagree and, unlike a teenager, you know when to let things go.

Both these periods can be happy times, but I look back at my own teenage years with no desire to go back. Adult life may be less dramatic, but fireworks don't keep you warm.

Sample answer sheets

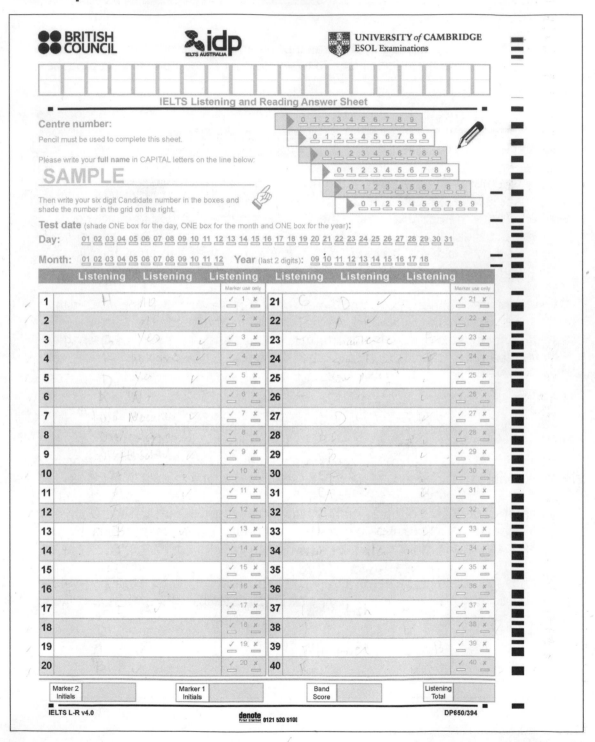

Please write your **full name** in CAPITAL letters on the line below:

SAMPLE

Please write your Candidate number on the line below:

Please write your three digit language code in the boxes and shade the numbers in the grid on the right.

	0 1 2 3 4 5 6 7 8 9
	0 1 2 3 4 5 6 7 8 9
	0 1 2 3 4 5 6 7 8 9

Are you: Female? ▢ Male? ▢

Reading Reading Reading Reading Reading Reading

Module taken (shade one box): Academic ▢ General Training ▢

		Marker use only			Marker use only
1		✓ 1 ✗	**21**		✓ 21 ✗
2		✓ 2 ✗	**22**		✓ 22 ✗
3		✓ 3 ✗	**23**		✓ 23 ✗
4		✓ 4 ✗	**24**		✓ 24 ✗
5		✓ 5 ✗	**25**		✓ 25 ✗
6		✓ 6 ✗	**26**		✓ 26 ✗
7		✓ 7 ✗	**27**		✓ 27 ✗
8		✓ 8 ✗	**28**		✓ 28 ✗
9		✓ 9 ✗	**29**		✓ 29 ✗
10		✓ 10 ✗	**30**		✓ 30 ✗
11		✓ 11 ✗	**31**		✓ 31 ✗
12		✓ 12 ✗	**32**		✓ 32 ✗
13		✓ 13 ✗	**33**		✓ 33 ✗
14		✓ 14 ✗	**34**		✓ 34 ✗
15		✓ 15 ✗	**35**		✓ 35 ✗
16		✓ 16 ✗	**36**		✓ 36 ✗
17		✓ 17 ✗	**37**		✓ 37 ✗
18		✓ 18 ✗	**38**		✓ 38 ✗
19		✓ 19 ✗	**39**		✓ 39 ✗
20		✓ 20 ✗	**40**		✓ 40 ✗

Marker 2 Initials		Marker 1 Initials		Band Score		Reading Total	

Acknowledgements

The authors and publishers acknowledge the following sources of copyright material and are grateful for the permissions granted. While every effort has been made, it has not always been possible to identify the sources of all the material used, or to trace all copyright holders. If any omissions are brought to our notice, we will be happy to include the appropriate acknowledgements on reprinting.

Ray P. Norris for the text on pp. 22–23 adapted from 'Is there anybody out there?' by Ray P. Norris, Australia Telescope National Facility, *Current Affairs Bulletin*, October 1993. Reproduced with permission; Guardian News and Media Ltd for the text on pp. 25–26 adapted from 'The giant turtle's tale' by Richard Dawkins, *The Guardian*, 20.02.03. Copyright © Guardian News & Media Ltd 2003; Stuart J. McLaren for the text on pp. 41–42 adapted from 'Noise in Classrooms and the Effect on Children with Auditory Function Deficit' by Stuart J. McLaren. Reproduced with permission; Immediate Media Company Bristol Limited for the text on pp. 45–46 adapted from 'Venus in Transit' copyright © Heather Couper and Nigel Henbest, original text from *Focus Magazine*, June 2004. Copyright © Immediate Media Company Bristol Limited; Harvard Business Publishing for the text on pp. 49–50 adapted from *Iconoclast: A Neuroscientist Reveals How to Think Differently* by Gregory Berns, Harvard Business Publishing, 2008. Reproduced with permission; Cambridge University Press for the text on pp. 63–64 adapted from *The Cambridge Encyclopedia of the English Language 2nd edition* by David Crystal, 2003. Copyright © Cambridge University Press 1995, 2003. Reprinted with permission of Cambridge University Press and David Crystal; Guardian News and Media Ltd for the text on pp. 67–68 adapted from 'Electricity from under the sea' by Paul Brown, *The Guardian*, 10.02.03. Copyright © Guardian News & Media Ltd 2003; Immediate Media Company Bristol Limited for the text on pp. 71–72 adapted from 'The Big Idea' copyright © Robert Matthews, original text from *Focus Magazine*, June 2004. Copyright © Immediate Media Company Bristol Limited; United Nations for the text on p. 76 adapted from 'Population: youngest and oldest countries for 2000 and 2050', United Nations Population Division. Reproduced with permission; Encyclopædia Britannica for the text on pp. 87–88 adapted from 'Marie Curie'. Adapted with permission from Encyclopædia Britannica. Copyright © 2012 by Encyclopædia Britannica, Inc; Wiley-Blackwell and The Open University for the text on pp. 91–92 adapted from *Children's Personal and Social Development* by Sharon Ding and Karen Littleton, Wiley-Blackwell and The Open University. Reproduced with permission; Bloomsbury Publishing for the text on pp. 97–98 adapted from *Heritage, Tourism and Society* by David T. Herbert, published by Continuum, 1997. Reproduced with permission; U.S. Energy Information Administration for the text on p. 101 adapted from 'Annual Energy Outlook: Energy Consumption by Fuel, 1980–2030', U.S. Energy Information Administration, 2007. Reproduced with permission; About.com for the text on p. 109 adapted from 'A formal, professional dress code' by Susan M. Heathfield, About.com, 26.05.08. Copyright © 2012 Susan M. Heathfield, http://humanresources.about.com. Used with permission of About Inc. which can be found online at www.about.com. All rights reserved; John Lewis Partnership for the text on p. 111 adapted from 'John Lewis Benefits', www.jlpjobs.com. Reproduced with permission; Settlement.org for the text on p. 122 adapted from 'Why should I get my international educational credentials evaluated? ' by World Education Services, www.settlement.org. Reproduced with permission; Oxford University Press Canada for the text on p. 124 adapted from *You're Hired… Now What?* by Lynda Goldman, 2010. Reproduced with permission of Oxford University Press Canada; NI Syndication Limited for the text on p. 126–127 adapted from 'To infinity and beyond: the plane-less pilot' by John-Paul Flintoff and John Follain, *The Times* 18.05.08. Copyright © NI Syndication Limited.

Photo acknowledgements

The authors and publishers acknowledge the following sources of photographs and are grateful for the permissions granted.

p. 22: Jut/Shutterstock; p. 45: Eckhard Slawik/Science Photo Library; p. 87: Sueddeutsche Zeitung Photo/Mary Evans; p. 107: John Peter Photography/Alamy.